McGRAW-HILL
Language
Arts

PRACTICE

Mc
Graw
Hill
Education

CONTENTS GRADE 4

UNIT **1** SENTENCES AND PERSONAL NARRATIVE

GRAMMAR SENTENCES

BUILD SKILLS

WRITING PERSONAL NARRATIVE

UNIT ② NOUNS AND WRITING THAT COMPARES

GRAMMAR NOUNS

BUILD SKILLS

WRITING WRITING THAT COMPARES

McGraw-Hill School Division

UNIT ③ VERBS AND PERSUASIVE WRITING

GRAMMAR VERBS

BUILD SKILLS

WRITING PERSUASIVE WRITING

McGraw-Hill School Division

UNIT (4) ADJECTIVES AND EXPLANATORY WRITING

McGraw-Hill School Division

UNIT (5) PRONOUNS AND WRITING A STORY

McGraw-Hill School Division

UNIT 5 PRONOUNS AND WRITING A STORY

UNIT ⑥ ADVERBS, PREPOSITIONS, AND EXPOSITORY WRITING

GRAMMAR   ADVERBS AND PREPOSITIONS

BUILD SKILLS

WRITING   EXPOSITORY WRITING

McGraw-Hill School Division

Sentences

> **REMEMBER** THE **RULES**
> - A **sentence** is a group of words that expresses a complete thought.
>   *Nitza writes to her pen pal.*
> - A **sentence fragment** is a group of words that does not express a complete thought.
>   *Her pen pal.*

A. Underline each sentence.

1. I am a good writer.

2. We send messages using a secret code.

3. Only Nitza and I.

4. I visited my pen pal's school.

5. Her friends were very nice to me.

6. Hugged and hugged.

7. We walked home through the park.

8. She also writes to a pen pal in New Mexico.

9. On the envelope.

10. With my pen pal.

B. Tell which group of words are sentences. Write *sentence*.

11. Ran to the door. _____

12. I called her on the telephone. _____

13. She was delighted to hear my voice. _____

14. Nitza and I talked for one hour. _____

15. Got very worried. _____

At Home: Write three sentences about yourself to a pen pal or a classmate. Does each sentence express a complete thought?

1

Declarative and Interrogative Sentences

┌─ **REMEMBER** THE **RULES** ─────────────────────────────────
│
│ • A **declarative sentence** makes a statement. It ends with a **period (.).**
│   *My pen pal wrote a funny story.*
│ • An **interrogative sentence** asks a question. It ends with a **question mark (?).**
│   *Would you like to have a pen pal?*
└──

A. Write **D** if the sentence is declarative. Write **I** if the sentence is interrogative.

1. A pen pal can be from another country. _____

2. What sports do children in other lands play? _____

3. You write your pen pal about yourself. _____

4. A friendship with a pen pal can last forever. _____

5. How many children in your class have pen pals? _____

B. Rewrite each sentence. Use a capital letter and a period (.) or a question mark (?).

6. thanon, my pen pal, lives in Thailand

   _____

7. his school is the biggest building in the village

   _____

8. does he wear a school uniform

   _____

9. how do Thai children greet grown-ups

   _____

10. children may put their palms together and bow

    _____

At Home: Find an interesting picture in a book or magazine. Write a statement about it. Then write a question about it.

McGraw-Hill Language Arts
Grade 4, Unit 1, Sentences,
pages 4–5 /10

McGraw-Hill School Division

Imperative and Exclamatory Sentences

> **REMEMBER** THE **RULES**
>
> - An **imperative sentence** tells or asks someone to do something. It ends with a **period (.)**.
>   *Stir-fry the food quickly.*
> - An **exclamatory sentence** shows strong feeling. It ends with an **exclamation mark (!)**.
>   *That food smells wonderful!*

A. Write **IM** if the sentence is imperative. Write **E** if the sentence is exclamatory.

1. Place the wok on the stove, please. _____

2. Pour peanut oil into the pan. _____

3. How hot the oil is! _____

4. What fun we are having! _____

5. Add the bean sprouts, snow peas, and broccoli. _____

B. Rewrite each sentence. Use a capital letter and a period (.) or an exclamation mark (!).

6. put the loaves of bread on the shelf

_____

7. look at this rye bread

_____

8. what a terrific baker you are

_____

9. give these two loaves to Mr. Brown

_____

10. you are a great helper

_____

McGraw-Hill School Division

At Home: Write three sentences. Tell someone what steps to follow to make a sandwich. Write your directions as imperative sentences.

Combining Sentences: Compound Sentences

> **REMEMBER THE RULES**
>
> • A **compound sentence** contains two sentences joined by a comma (,) and the conjuction *and*, *or*, or *but*.
>
>   *I ride my bike to school,* **but** *other students ride the bus.*

A. Read each pair of sentences. Circle the conjunction you would use to join the sentences.

1. After school I biked to Mike's house. I knocked on the door.   **and**   **or**   **but**

2. Stop your bicycle. Wait for the traffic light to change.   **and**   **or**   **but**

3. I started to pedal. My bike didn't move.   **and**   **or**   **but**

4. Should we go bicycle riding today? Should we roller-skate?   **and**   **or**   **but**

5. Some people prefer bikes with wide tires. Others like bikes with thin tires.   **and**   **or**   **but**

B. Write *sentence* or *compound sentence* next to each sentence.

6. Wear a bicycle helmet, and watch the

   traffic. _____

7. Bicycle riding is good exercise, but some _____
   people prefer jogging.

8. My friend went home after he hurt his ankle. _____

9. Is this a bike path, or is this path for walkers only?

   _____

10. Ray and I look forward to riding our bicycles another day.

   _____

At Home: Write two related sentences about a sport you enjoy and then use *and*, *or*, or *but* to join them.

**McGraw-Hill Language Arts
Grade 4, Unit 1, Sentences,
pages 8–9**

4   /10

Mechanics and Usage: Sentence Punctuation

REMEMBER THE RULES

- Every sentence must begin with a **capital letter.**
- **Declarative** and **imperative** sentences end with **periods.**
- An **interrogative** sentence ends with a **question mark.**
- An **exclamatory** sentence ends with an **exclamation mark.**
- A **comma** is used before *and, or,* or *but* in a **compound** sentence.

A. Make each sentence correct. Add the correct end punctuation or a comma. Use a red pencil or pen.

1. Please save me a seat or I will stand in the back of the auditorium.

2. The musicians are already on stage

3. Are you enjoying the contest

4. Wow, the singer is fabulous

5. My family attended the contest and later we all went to a restaurant.

B. Write five sentences about the kind of music you enjoy. Use one of each of the four kinds of sentences. Then write one compound sentence.

6. _____

_____

7. _____

_____

8. _____

_____

9. _____

_____

10. _____

_____

McGraw-Hill Language Arts
Grade 4, Unit 1, Sentences,
pages 10–11

At Home: Look through a magazine to find examples of declarative, imperative, interrogative, and exclamatory sentences.

Mixed Review

┌─ **REMEMBER** THE **RULES** ═══════════════════════════════

- A **declarative sentence** makes a statement. It ends with a
  period. *We are going to see the circus.*

- An **interrogative sentence** asks a question. It ends with a **question
  mark.** *How many people will be going with us?*

- An **imperative sentence** tells or asks someone to do something. It
  ends in a **period.** *Come with me to buy the tickets.*

- An **exclamatory sentence** shows strong feeling. It ends with an
  exclamation mark. *That's a great act!*

- A **compound sentence** is made up of two sentences joined by a
  comma (,) and a **conjunction**, such as *and, or,* or *but.*

A. Write whether each sentence is *declarative, interrogative, imperative,* or
exclamatory. Add the correct end punctuation to each sentence.

1. Isn't it time for the circus to come to town _____

2. Buy a ticket for each of us _____

3. Should I get tickets for this weekend _____

4. Check to see if everyone can go then _____

5. The tickets I bought are right next to the ring _____

6. A tall man in a costume announced the acts _____

7. The woman on the trapeze is so strong _____

B. Write each pair of sentences as a compound sentence. Use a comma
and *and, but,* or *or* to combine them.

8. The circus is finally here. We can hardly wait to go.

_____

9. Mike went last week. We are going this weekend.

_____

10. Will your mother take us? Should we go on the bus?

_____

At Home: Talk to family members about a place you have all
been to together. Write one declarative, one interrogative, one
imperative, one exclamatory, and one compound sentence.

McGraw-Hill Language Arts
Grade 4, Unit 1, Mixed Review,
pages 12–13

10

Complete Subjects and Complete Predicates

REMEMBER THE RULES

- The **subject** part of a sentence tells what the subject is about. The **complete subject** includes all the words in the subject.
- The **predicate** part of a sentence tells what the subject does or is. The **complete predicate** includes all the words in the predicate.

My cousin Ramon *visits us next week.*

↑   ↑

complete subject   complete predicate

A. Draw one line under each complete subject. Draw two lines under each complete predicate.

1. Ramon travels to many countries for his job.

2. My mother will meet him at the airport.

3. He sometimes stays at our home.

4. Ramon brought us presents from Holland last year.

5. My family enjoys hearing about Ramon's adventures.

B. Write the complete subject or the complete predicate for each sentence.

6. My cousin's favorite place is the Galapagos Islands.

   Complete Predicate: _____

7. The islands are in the Pacific Ocean.

   Complete Subject: _____

8. Giant tortoises are found only on the Galapagos Islands.

   Complete Subject: _____

9. These big reptiles can live to be 100 years old.

   Complete Predicate: _____

10. Marine iguanas make their home on these islands, too.

    Complete Subject: _____

McGraw-Hill Language Arts
Grade 4, Unit 1, Sentences,
10 | **pages 14–15**

At Home: Write three sentences about a place you visited.
Draw one line under each complete subject and two lines
under each complete predicate.

7

Simple Subjects

┌─ **REMEMBER** THE **RULES** ═══════════════════════════

• The **simple subject** tells exactly who or what the sentence is about.

My butterfly <u>kite</u> soars above us.

↑

simple subject
└───

A. Circle the simple subject in each sentence.

1. The annual kite contest takes place this weekend.

2. Fifty contestants are competing for first prize this year.

3. The rules require that each contestant make his or her own kite.

4. Last year I made a beautiful red box kite.

5. Nine other people also made box kites.

6. Others built diamond, delta, and various kinds of huge kites.

7. A strong wind can blow and snap the string on a kite.

8. Many great kites were lost this time.

9. A fifteen-year-old girl was awarded first prize—a brand-new kite.

10. Children around the world fly kites just for fun.

B. Choose a simple subject from the box to complete each sentence.

men	he	kite	soldiers	general

11. About a thousand years ago, a _____ won a battle with a kite.

12. Did _____ tie a lantern to a kite?

13. The odd-looking _____ flew above the enemy camp.

14. Many enemy _____ saw the strange yellow light.

15. All the _____ threw down their weapons.

At Home: Choose five sentences from your favorite story. Read them aloud to a parent or guardian. Then point out the simple subject in each sentence.

8

McGraw-Hill Language Arts Grade 4, Unit 1, Sentences, pages 16–17 /15

McGraw-Hill School Division

Simple Predicates

┌─ **REMEMBER** THE **RULES** ════════════════════════════
│
│ • The **simple predicate** tells exactly what the subject does or is.
│   *Nature <u>provides</u> people with renewable resources.*
│   ↑
│   **simple predicate**
│
└──

A. Circle the simple predicate in each sentence.

1. Renewable resources include air and water.

2. Some people pollute our air and water.

3. Nonrenewable resources existed a long, long time ago.

4. The remains of plant and animal life became renewable resources.

5. Over a period of millions of years, these remains turned into oil, coal, and gas.

6. Coal supplies about 30 percent of the world's energy.

7. Natural gas heats homes and factories.

8. Offshore oil wells transport oil from deep in the ground.

9. Oil comes from plants and animals, too.

10. These plants and animals lived millions of years ago.

B. Choose a simple predicate from the box to complete each sentence.

holds	destroy	make	comes	exists

11. The largest rain forest in the world _____ in South America.

12. The Amazon rain forest _____ millions of trees.

13. Trees _____ oxygen.

14. Many people _____ thousands of trees every year.

15. Sixty percent of the world's oxygen _____ from the Amazon.

15 **McGraw-Hill Language Arts**
Grade 4, Unit 1, Sentences,
pages 18–19

At Home: Choose five sentences from a magazine or newspaper article. Read them aloud to a parent or guardian. Then point out the simple predicate in each sentence.

9

Combining Sentences: Compound Subjects

┌─ **REMEMBER** THE **RULES** ─────────────────────────────┐

• A **compound subject** contains two or more simple subjects that have the same predicate.

    My brother and I take our dog for a walk.
         ↑

    compound subject

└──┘

A. Underline the compound subject in each sentence. Circle the conjunction that joins the subjects.

  1. Dad and I always cook dinner on weekends.

  2. Broiled fish or broiled chicken is our specialty.

  3. Mom or Tomás washes the dishes after dinner.

  4. Saturdays and Sundays are my favorite days of the week.

  5. My uncle and my cousin join us for card games.

B. Circle the subject in each sentence. Then combine the subjects to write a new sentence. Use *and* or *or.*

  6. My brother unpacks the groceries. My sister unpacks the groceries.

_____

  7. Tomatoes go into my spaghetti sauce. Peppers go into my spaghetti sauce.

_____

  8. Apples fill the big blue fruit bowl. Pears fill the big blue fruit bowl.

_____

  9. The snow kept our guests away. The cold kept our guests away.

_____

10. Luisa will serve the dessert. Tony will serve the dessert.

_____

At Home: Combine these two sentences by creating a compound subject: *My parents like to play games after dinner. I like to play games after dinner.*

McGraw-Hill Language Arts
Grade 4, Unit 1, Sentences,
pages 20–21   /**10**

Combining Sentences: Compound Predicates

┌───┐
REMEMBER THE RULES

- A **compound predicate** contains two or more simple predicates.
- The **conjunction** *and, or,* or *but* is used to join the words in a compound predicate.

  Today our class <u>reads</u> (and) <u>learns about the sea</u>.
  ↑
  compound predicate
└───┘

A. Circle the conjunction that joins the compound predicate.

1. Many people live and work on the sea.

2. Fishers on ships haul and process fresh fish.

3. Ultrasound equipment finds and locates fish underwater.

4. We must dramatize or write a story about the sea.

5. I can draw or paint the scenery for our play.

B. Underline the simple predicate in each sentence. Then combine the predicates to write a new sentence. Use *and, or,* or *but.*

6. A lobster fisher empties a lobster pot. A lobster fisher cleans a lobster pot.

   _____

7. A navigator on a cruise ship understands computers. A navigator on a cruise ship uses computers.

   _____

8. The Coast Guard didn't protect those people. The Coast Guard rescued those people.

   _____

9. Marine biologists study the land beneath the sea. Marine biologists investigate the land beneath the sea.

   _____

10. We clap our hands for the best story. We raise our hands for the best story.

    _____

McGraw-Hill Language Arts
Grade 4, Unit 1, Sentences,
10 **pages 22–23**

At Home: Combine these two sentences by creating a
compound predicate: *The audience cheered the performers.*
The audience applauded the performers.

11

Mechanics and Usage: Correcting Run-on Sentences

REMEMBER THE **RULES**

- A **run-on sentence** joins two or more sentences that should stand alone or be joined with a comma and the word *and*, *but*, or *or*.

  Run-on: *Scientists believe that millions of years ago fish had armor they had no jaws like the fish today.*

  Correct: *Scientists believe that millions of years ago fish had armor, and they had no jaws like the fish today.*

A. Circle the run-on sentences.

1. Many kinds of fish form schools. They don't learn anything.

2. There may be only a few fish in a school, or there may be hundreds.

3. A school of fish is an amazing sight they act as one.

4. They all head in the same direction they all swim at the same speed.

5. Fish in schools are in less danger it is easier for them to find food.

B. Rewrite each run-on sentence as two sentences or a compound sentence.

6. Most fish are about a foot long some fish are giants.

_____

7. Some of the biggest fish are sharks the very biggest is the whale shark.

_____

8. It may be 60 feet long it may weigh 30,000 pounds.

_____

9. Another big fish is the manta ray this fish looks like a weird, flying creature.

_____

10. The ocean sunfish seems to be all head it is often called a *headfish*.

_____

At Home: Correct each run-on sentence in Part A.

McGraw-Hill Language Arts
Grade 4, Unit 1, Sentences,
pages 24–25

12

/10

McGraw-Hill School Division

Mixed Review

┌─ **REMEMBER** THE **RULES** ─────────────────────────────
- The **complete subject** includes all the words in the subject.
  All kinds of dogs are at the dog show.
- The **complete predicate** includes all the words in the predicate.
  *The dog show **comes to town once a year.***
- A **compound subject** contains two or more simple subjects that have the same predicate. ***Dog and cat shows** are very popular.*
- A **compound predicate** contains two or more simple predicates that have the same subject. *The dogs **run and bark at the show.***
└──

A. Circle the complete subject. Underline the complete predicate.

1. The dog show begins this weekend.

2. This popular event lasts for a whole week.

3. My family and I are going on the last day.

4. Dogs from all over the world compete in the show.

5. Every recognized breed has its own contest.

6. A ribbon and trophy go to the best of each breed.

7. The big event happens on the last day.

B. Write each pair of sentences as one sentence by forming a compound subject or a compound predicate.

8. Fox terriers are my favorite dogs. Basset hounds are my favorite dogs.

   _____

9. The judges watch the dogs carefully. The judges examine the dogs carefully.

   _____

10. The terriers jump at each other. The terriers bark at each other.

   _____

10 **McGraw-Hill Language Arts**
Grade 4, Unit 1, Mixed Review,
pages 26–27

At Home: Write five sentences about a dog in your family or a dog you know. Circle the complete subject. Underline the complete predicate.

13

Common Errors: Sentence Fragments and Run-on Sentences

REMEMBER THE **RULES**

- Correct a **sentence fragment** by adding a subject or a predicate.

    Has very long legs for running.

    The large ostrich has very long legs for running.

- Correct a **run-on sentence** by rewriting it as two sentences or as a compound sentence.

    Once I saw an ostrich at the zoo it is the world's largest bird.

    Once I saw an ostrich at the zoo. It is the world's largest bird.

A. Rewrite each group of words as two separate sentences or as a compound sentence.

An ostrich egg is about seven inches long it weighs three pounds. Hatches in six weeks chicks grow a foot per month. Adult ostriches can be up to six feet tall they live in groups on the plains. Their bodies are heavy and their wings are short. They cannot fly they can run as fast as a horse.

_____

_____

_____

_____

_____

B. Add a subject or predicate to each group of words.

6. _____ live on the plains.

7. Ostriches_____.

8. The largest egg _____.

9. _____ weighs three pounds.

10. _____ runs very fast.

At Home: Write a paragraph about an interesting animal. Then check your writing for run-on sentences and sentence fragments.

14

McGraw-Hill Language Arts **Grade 4, Unit 1, Sentences, pages 28–29**

/10

Study Skills: Note-Taking and Summarizing

> To recall important information
> - **take notes** using words, phrases, or full sentences.
> - include **main ideas** with their **supporting details** in your notes.
> - write a **summary** stating the main idea and supporting details.

A. Read the paragraph about glaciers. Then look at the notes. For each note, circle **main idea** or **detail.**

Beginning in the Ice Age, millions of years ago, the earth formed glaciers—that is, large masses of ice. Everything in their path—trees, fields, valleys—became buried. Mountains, rocks, and pebbles were crushed when a glacier moved over them. What was left on the ground afterward was a powder, or silt. As a glacier moved, it sometimes split at a crevasse. Each split that caused a crevasse made a huge booming sound that could be heard for miles. A little chunk of ice that broke off a glacier became an iceberg. It was an iceberg, for example, that caused the famous 1912 sinking of the *Titanic,* a great passenger ship. Icebergs and glaciers still occupy northern regions of the earth.

1. millions of years ago: Ice Age   **main idea**   **detail**

2. large mass of ice: glacier   **main idea**   **detail**

3. crushed rocks, mountains: silt   **main idea**   **detail**

4. split in glacier: crevasse   **main idea**   **detail**

5. small chunk of glacier: iceberg   **main idea**   **detail**

B. Determine whether the statements below are true (T) or false (F). Circle the correct answer.

6. The main idea of the paragraph talks about glaciers.   T   F

7. Glaciers were formed thousands of years ago.   T   F

8. Glaciers make a loud noise when splitting apart.   T   F

9. Huge chunks of ice from glaciers are called *silt.*   T   F

10. The *Titanic* sunk after hitting an iceberg.   T   F

McGraw-Hill Language Arts
Grade 4, Unit 1, Study Skills,
pages 36–37
10

At Home: Take notes and write a summary of a newspaper or magazine article that interests you.

15

Vocabulary: Time-Order Words

- A **time-order word** tells when things happen and in what order. Sometimes a group of words is used to tell time order.

  Tomorrow we are going to put new chains on my bike.

A. Read each sentence. Write the time-order word or words on the line.

1. The girls' gymnastic class meets after school.

   _____

2. The boys' gymnastic class meets before art.

   _____

3. First, we do stretching exercises, and then, we do broad jumps.

   _____

4. Next, we work on the trampoline. _____

5. Finally, we get to swing on the rings. _____

B. Choose a word from the box to complete each sentence. Then rewrite the sentence on the line.

before	finally	first	next	then

6. _____ planning a party, get permission from parents.

   _____

7. The _____ thing to do is make a guest list.

   _____

8. _____, you might make invitations.

   _____

9. _____, you can decide on a theme for your party.

   _____

10. _____, choose food, decorations, and games to play.

    _____

At Home: Write a paragraph explaining how to make pizza. Use time-order words.

16

McGraw-Hill Language Arts
Grade 4, Unit 1, Vocabulary,
pages 38–39 /10

McGraw-Hill School Division

Composition: Main Idea

> - The main idea is usually stated in a **topic sentence** and tells what the piece of writing is about.
> - **Supporting details** help to develop or clarify the main idea.
> - Take out any detail sentence that does not have anything important to say about the main idea.
> - Put the main idea and the supporting ideas in the most sensible order.
> - Use words like *next, first,* or *finally* to connect ideas in a paragraph.

A. Read the paragraph. Use the numbers to answer the questions.

   (1) Without my cat Paws, my mother and I would never have found the key to an old trunk full of family photographs. (2) My mother first looked in every drawer in the house, but no keys appeared. (3) Next, she asked me to look behind the couch in the living room, but still no keys appeared. (4) She was about to give up, and I was afraid I'd never get to see the pictures of my family. (5) Finally, when we thought all was lost, my mother and I found Paws swatting at a shiny silver key under the kitchen table.

1. Which sentence is the topic sentence? _____

2. Which sentences develop the main idea with supporting details?_____

What three words does the writer use to connect ideas?

3. _____   **4.** _____   **5.** _____

B. Use the instructions in parentheses to complete the sentences. Use your imagination!

6. (Main idea/topic sentence) I was sad when I realized _____ was lost.

7. (Time-order word) _____, I looked in every room of the house.

8. Next, (supporting detail) _____

9. Then, (supporting detail) _____

10. Finally, I found it (supporting detail) _____

McGraw-Hill Language Arts
Grade 4, Unit 1, Composition Skills,
pages 40–41

At Home: Write a paragraph about a favorite photograph of you or someone you know. Develop your topic sentence and supporting sentences using the information from the box at the top of this page.

17

10

McGraw-Hill School Division

Features of a Personal Narrative

A good personal narrative
- tells a story from **personal experience.**
- expresses the **writer's feelings** using the *I* point of view.
- has an interesting **beginning, middle,** and **end.**
- uses **time-order words** to show sequence of events.

A. Read each of the following narratives. Circle the time-order words that show the sequence of events.

1. The sky became dark. I asked my older brother, "How far are we from home?" First, Carl protected me under a large umbrella that he held above us both. Then, he told me that we were almost home. The wind nearly whisked my small, five-year-old body off the sidewalk. Carl and I looked toward the end of the avenue. The sky began to clear. Finally, what we saw was not darkness but a colorful rainbow.

2. Try, try again. That was the saying my father told me when I lost at a board game. My aunt gave me a great board game for my ninth birthday. First, I challenged my seven-year-old sister to play the game. She preferred to draw. Next, I asked my father to play with me, and he did. Well, he won all the games we played until just a few weeks ago. Finally, I discovered a winning strategy, and it paid off. When I asked my father to play, he smiled and said, "You're good enough to teach your sister."

B. Use the information from the narratives to answer the following questions.

3. What interesting event happens at the end of the first personal narrative?

   _____

4. How do you think the writer feels at the beginning of the narrative? At the end of the narrative?

   _____

5. How does the second personal narrative begin?

   _____

At Home: Make a list of experiences about which you could write a personal narrative. Choose one experience and **17a** write a detail for the beginning, middle, and ending.

McGraw-Hill Language Arts
Grade 4, Unit 1, Personal Narrative,
pages 48–49

5

McGraw-Hill School Division

Prewrite: Personal Narrative

A **personal narrative** is a true story about yourself. The events in a narrative happen in a certain order, or sequence. To help you begin a personal narrative, it is a good idea to organize your thoughts. A **sequence chart** can help.

Plan your own personal narrative. Think about a personal experience you would like to share with others. Then organize your ideas. Think about what happened first, second, and third. You might end your narrative by explaining how the experience made you feel or what you learned from it.

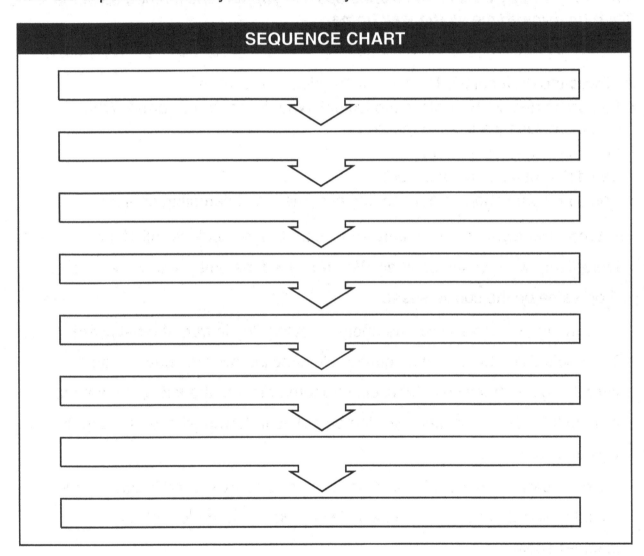

SEQUENCE CHART

CHECKLIST
- Have you listed important parts of the narrative?
- Are the details listed in logical order?
- Do you need to do any research?

McGraw-Hill Language Arts
Grade 4, Unit 1, Personal Narrative,
pages 50–51

At Home: Think of a person who may be able to help you add details to your narrative. List questions you might ask this person.

17b

Revise: Personal Narrative

You can improve your personal narrative by including important ideas and details. This is known as elaborating. When you **revise** your writing, include your feelings about the event.

Draft: *When I left school, I saw a puppy alone on the steps. He jumped up at me and followed me.*

Revision: *When I left school **on Friday,** I saw a **brown and white** puppy **with long, floppy ears** on the **front** steps. He **yapped** and jumped up at me. **Then he** followed me **all the way home.***

A. Read the draft below. Then follow the steps to revise it.

• Add some details. How old is the writer? What is the dog's name? What kind of cookies were being made?

• Add some time-order words.

• Use different types of sentences.

• Combine some short sentences to make one long interesting sentence.

When I was young, my granny and I were baking cookies. All of the ingredients were on the counter. We had mixed the batter and were ready to drop some on the cookie sheet.

Grandma went to answer the phone. I let the dog in from the backyard. The dog's paws were on the counter. He knocked over the batter onto the floor. He got batter all over himself. Grandma ran into the kitchen. I went to pick up the bowl. I knocked over the bag of flour. It was all over the dog. It was all over me, too.

I was scared. I thought I would be scolded. Granny started laughing, and so did I. Grandpa came in. He said, "When did the tornado hit?" We all laughed again.

B. Write the new paragraphs on a separate piece of paper.

At Home: Write your own paragraph about baking cookies or some other cooking experience you've had. Then revise your work.

17c

McGraw-Hill Language Arts
Grade 4, Unit 1, Personal Narrative,
pages 56–59

McGraw-Hill School Division

Proofread: Personal Narrative

PROOFREADING MARKS

⌗ new paragraph

∧ add

ℒ take out

≡ Make a capital letter.

╱ Make a small letter.

ⓢⓟ Check the spelling.

⊙ Add a period.

After you revise your narrative, you will need to **proofread** it to correct any errors.

When you proofread a personal narrative, you should:
- Indent paragraphs.
- Correct spelling mistakes.
- Include punctuation for every sentence.
- Add commas before *and, or,* or *but* in compound sentences.
- Correct run-on sentences.

A. Read the following personal narrative. Use the proofreading marks from the box to mark any errors you find. You can use the "add" mark to show where punctuation marks should go.

One Sunday afternoon, my Dad took me to a

baseball game he bought me a cap a hot dog, and

a soda What a game it was Our team finally hit a

home run in the ninth inning but so did the other

team. Did you hear me yell when we won that

game The best part came when I got my favorite

player's autograph I was so happy!

B. Use the corrections you marked to rewrite the paragraph on another piece of paper.

10 **McGraw-Hill Language Arts** Grade 4, Unit 1, Personal Narrative, pages 60–61

At Home: Look in a dictionary for more proofreading marks. Try to learn two new ones.

17d

Nouns

REMEMBER THE **RULES**

- A **noun** names a person, place, or thing.

  *The **geologist** talks about **glaciers** at the **university**.*

  ↕   ↕   ↕

  person   **thing**   **place**

A. Write *person*, *place*, or *thing* to identify the underlined noun.

1. My Uncle David is a <u>professor</u> of geology. _____

2. He said parts of <u>North America</u> once had many glaciers. _____

3. A glacier is a giant <u>mass</u> of moving ice. _____

4. Some glaciers form when snow accumulates in a high mountain

   <u>valley</u>. _____

5. This type of glacier is called a valley <u>glacier</u>. _____

B. Underline the nouns in each sentence.

6. Eventually the ice thickens into a thick, frozen sheet.

7. Pressure from the weight of the glacier causes it to move.

8. The moving glacier rubs against the bottom and sides of the valley.

9. The glacier picks up and carries rocks and sediment as it moves.

10. The land is eroded to form a wide U-shaped valley.

11. A moving glacier leaves behind piles of hard bedrock.

12. A geologist can use the scratches to tell the direction of movement.

13. Sometimes loose sediment is deposited at the edges of the glacier.

14. These mounds of sediment are called moraines.

15. Scientists use these hilly formations to tell where a glacier stopped.

At Home: Underline at least one other noun in each sentence in Part A.

Singular and Plural Nouns

┌─ **REMEMBER** THE **RULES** ═══════════════════════════════════

- A **singular noun** names one person, place, or thing.
- A **plural noun** names more than one person, place, or thing.

        one **girl** → *two* **girls**

        one **gas** → *two* **gases**

        one **bench** → *two* **benches**

└───

A. Write *singular* or *plural* to identify the underlined noun.

1. You will need a pack of <u>matches</u> to light the grill. _____

2. The old <u>ashes</u> can remain in the bottom of the grill. _____

3. A <u>bus</u> with campers will arrive very soon. _____

4. Each camper will need a <u>dish</u>, a spoon, and a fork. _____

5. They will be taking <u>classes</u> in archery and swimming. _____

B. Underline the singular noun in each sentence. Write the plural form of the noun you underlined. You may need to change some sentences to make them grammatically correct.

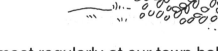

6. Scouts meet regularly at our town hall. _____

7. They are planning several projects for the year ahead. _____

8. They want to replace the large bush near the front doors. _____

9. The overgrown plant will be difficult to remove. _____

10. Other nearby bushes had been chopped down with an ax. _____

11. The boys will be using ropes and a pulley this time. _____

12. The scout will need to use his muscles to pull it out. _____

13. The leader asked them to discuss other projects. _____

14. They talked about an empty lot that is several miles away. _____

15. The boys decided to build a playground there. _____

At Home: Write the singular and plural form of each underlined noun in Part A.

19

McGraw-Hill Language Arts
Grade 4, Unit 2, Nouns,
pages 90–91

15

Nouns Ending with *y*

REMEMBER THE RULES

- When a noun ends in a consonant + **y**, change the **y** to **i** and add **-es** to make the noun plural.

  one **hobby** → *two* **hobbies**

- When a noun ends in a vowel + **y**, add **-s** to make the noun plural.

  one **play** → *two* **plays**

A. Write the plural form of each singular noun.

1. toy _____
2. turkey _____
3. baby _____
4. story _____
5. day _____

6. ferry _____
7. cherry _____
8. dairy _____
9. galley _____
10. gallery _____

B. Write the plural form of the noun in parentheses.

11. Did you meet the new (lady)

   next door? _____

12. The one named Hannah has interesting

   (hobby). _____

13. The opera is one of her (joy). _____

14. Hannah's voice carries like a cage full of (canary). _____

15. She has been teaching me a lot about singing these (day). _____

16. She will take me to the opera over the (holiday). _____

17. An opera is often a story told through beautiful (song). _____

18. Only a few (city) present operas each year. _____

19. We will have to drive through two (valley) to get there. _____

20. Hannah has made (journey) like this many times before. _____

At Home: For each word in ( ) above, underline the letter that comes before the *y*. Tell which words need to change the *y* to *i* before adding *-es* to form the plural.

20

More Plural Nouns

┌─ **REMEMBER** THE **RULES** ══════════════════════════

- Some nouns have special plural forms. For example, singular nouns that end in *ife* have plurals that end in *ives* (wife/**wives**, life/**lives**, knife/**knives**).
- A few nouns have the same singular and plural forms. Many of these are animals (deer/**deer**, sheep/**sheep**, fish/**fish**, trout/**trout**, moose/**moose**).

A. Underline the correct plural form of each noun in dark type.

1. **foot**   foots, feet, footes
2. **knife**   knives, knifes, kniveys
3. **child**   childs, child, children
4. **trout**   trout, trouts, troutes
5. **ox**   ox, oxes, oxen

6. **catfish**   catfishes, catfish, catsfish
7. **deer**   deers, dears, deer
8. **tooth**   toothies, tooths, teeth
9. **mouse**   mice, mouses, mousen
10. **goose**   goose, geese, gooses

B. Write the plural form of the noun in parentheses to complete each sentence. Use a dictionary if you need help.

11. Many _____ study conservation, or the wise use of resources. (man)

12. _____ as well as men can be conservationists. (Woman)

13. Biologists can maintain _____ at a hatchery. (fish)

14. Conservationists can shelter herds of _____. (moose)

15. They may even count how many _____ live in an area. (mouse)

16. They can improve grazing lands for _____. (deer)

17. Overgrazing results when too many _____ graze in an area too long. (sheep)

18. Conservationists protect the _____ of endangered species. (life)

19. Once, flocks of _____ were a common sight. (goose)

20. Our _____ will need many resources. (child)

At Home: Write each singular noun from Part B and its plural form.

21

McGraw-Hill Language Arts
Grade 4, Unit 2, Nouns,
pages 94–95

⧄20

Common and Proper Nouns

REMEMBER THE RULES

- A **common noun** names any person, place, or thing.
- A **proper noun** names a special person, place, or thing. A proper noun always begins with a capital letter.

   *The **city** of **New York** is a gateway to our country.*

   common noun   proper noun   common noun   common noun

A. Write a common noun that could take the place of each proper noun.

1. Friday _____
2. April _____
3. Chicago _____
4. Earth _____
5. Europe _____

6. Eleanor Roosevelt _____
7. Presidents' Day _____
8. Mt. Everest _____
9. Pacific Ocean _____
10. Broadway Avenue _____

B. Write the letter of the **proper noun** that best completes the sentence.

11. Many citizens came to _____ from foreign countries.

   a. America   **b.** Countries

12. Some of the earliest settlers came to this country on a ship called

   the _____

   a. Mayflower   **b.** Boat

13. These people, called _____, were seeking their religious freedom.

   a. Puritans   **b.** Persons

14. Also known as the Pilgrims, they are remembered each _____ holiday.

   a. Immigrants   **b.** Thanksgiving

15. Many people left _____ because of new opportunities in America.

   a. Continent   **b.** Europe

At Home: Write the names of two holidays and the day and month on which they occur. For example, *Martin Luther King Jr. Day occurs on a Monday in January.*

Mechanics and Usage: Capitalization

REMEMBER THE RULES

- Capitalize the names of specific persons, places, things, days, months, and holidays.

  Main Street   Wednesday   October   Thanksgiving

- Capitalize family names and titles of respect.

  Governor Nelson

- Capitalize the first word and all important words in the titles of books, magazines, songs, poems, plays, short stories, and movies.

  Rip Van Winkle   Charlotte's Web

A. Rewrite each group of words correctly.

1. dr albert einstein _____

2. new york city _____

3. uncle bert _____

4. miss elaine barrett _____

5. the diary of a young girl _____

B. Rewrite each sentence using correct capitalization and punctuation.

6. My friend Caitlin volunteers at the local red cross.

_____

7. She is assigned to memorial hospital every tuesday.

_____

8. She delivers *reader's digest* and *newsweek* to the patients.

_____

9. A nurse named deb wallace introduced caitlin to the staff.

_____

10. caitlin received a thank-you note from mr and mrs ron arthur.

_____

At Home: Look in the newspaper for an advertisement about your favorite movie. Circle the date of the ad and the places the film is showing.

McGraw-Hill Language Arts
Grade 4, Unit 2, Nouns,
pages 98–99

� 10

Mixed Review

REMEMBER THE RULES

- A **singular noun** names one person, place, or thing.

    I like to visit may uncle's farm.

- A **plural noun** names more than one person, place, or thing. Add **-s** to form the plural of most nouns.

    There are many farms where I live.

- Add **-es** to form the plural of nouns ending in *s, x, ch,* or *sh.*

    This farmhouse has several porches.

- When a noun ends in a consonant followed by a *y*, change the *y* to *i* and add **-es** to make the plural.

    Many cities are surround by farms.

- A **proper noun** names a particular person, place, or thing and begins with a capital letter.

    Last August, Mr. Evens visited a farm in Colorado.

A. Write the plural form of each noun in parentheses.

1. Maria paints beautiful (picture) _____ of the country.

2. In one picture she painted two red (barn) _____.

3. You can see several (ox) _____ standing in the barnyard.

4. Look at the wild (canary) _____ in the picture.

5. You can almost hear them singing in the (branch) _____.

B. Write each sentence. Add capital letters where they are needed.

6. maria and I visited a farm in july.

7. We went on independence day weekend.

8. My father's friend mr. jacobs owns the michigan farm.

9. It is a typical example of a united states dairy farm.

10. mr. and mrs. jacobs moved to the farm from new york.

McGraw-Hill Language Arts
Grade 4, Unit 2, Mixed Review,
pages 100–101

At Home: Write five sentences about a relative you visited.
Include some singular, plural, and proper nouns. Circle all
the nouns you use.

10

24

Singular Possessive Nouns

┌─ **REMEMBER** THE **RULES** ════════════════════════════════

- A **singular possessive noun** is a singular noun that shows ownership.

- Form a singular possessive noun by adding an **apostrophe** and an **-s ('s)** to a singular noun.

    The boots of the soldier are made of leather.

    soldier + 's = soldier's

    *The **soldier's** boots are made of leather.*

A. Write the letter of the phrase from the box that correctly matches the given phrase.

1. soldiers of England _____

2. people of the colony _____

3. troops from Britain _____

4. freedom of a nation _____

5. harbor of Boston _____

a. a nations' freedom	f. Boston's harbor
b. a nation's freedom	g. Soldier's England
c. the colonies people	h. England's soldiers
d. the colony's people	i. Britain troop's
e. Bostons' harbors	j. Britain's troops

B. Rewrite each underlined phrase with a phrase that has a singular possessive noun.

6. At first, <u>colonists of America</u> were loyal to England.

_____

7. Yet in 1776, Americans rebelled against <u>the rule of the king</u>.

_____

8. The Revolution was in <u>the heart of each person</u>.

_____

9. <u>Laws of Britain</u> controlled the colonists.

_____

10. <u>Leaders of Boston</u> eventually organized the Boston Tea Party.

_____

McGraw-Hill School Division

25

At Home: How would you like to celebrate Independence Day? Complete this sentence: *My family's tradition for the 4th of July might be…*

McGraw-Hill Language Arts
Grade 4, Unit 2, Nouns,
pages 102–103   10

Plural Possessive Nouns

REMEMBER THE RULES

- A **plural possessive noun** is a plural noun that shows ownership.
  - the **students'** ideas
- Add an **apostrophe (')** to a plural noun that ends in **-s** to form the plural possessive.
  - the **citizens'** decision
- To form the plural possessive of a plural noun that does not end in **-s,** add an **apostrophe** and **-s ('s).**
  - the **children's** favorite

A. Write the correct plural possessive form of each underlined noun.

1. <u>leaders</u> speeches   _____

2. <u>women</u> opinions   _____

3. <u>committees</u> ideas   _____

4. <u>groups</u> decisions   _____

5. <u>candidates</u> roles   _____

B. Write another phrase for the underlined words.

6. <u>Rights of citizens</u> include the right to vote for a president.

_____

7. <u>Elections of all towns</u> are held on a Tuesday in November.

_____

8. It is the <u>privilege of people</u> to vote for a candidate.

_____

9. The <u>supporters of politicians</u> are usually Republican or Democrat.

_____

10. The <u>platforms of parties</u> are different.

_____

McGraw-Hill Language Arts
Grade 4, Unit 2, Nouns,
pages 104–105

10

At Home: Rewrite the sentences in Part B using the correct plural possessive noun.

26

Combining Sentences: Nouns

┌─ **REMEMBER** THE **RULES** ─────────────────────────────
- You can **combine sentences** that have similar ideas.
- You can combine nouns in the subject.

    Mary is baking cookies.   *Kathy is baking cookies.*

    Mary and Kathy are baking cookies.

- You can combine nouns in the predicate.

    Lynn is bringing napkins.   *Lynn is bringing plates.*

    Lynn is bringing napkins and plates.
└──

Write a combined sentence using the word in parentheses.

1. Are you planning a meeting? Are you planning an activity? (or)

   _____

2. Cara likes to get involved. Melissa likes to get involved. (and)

   _____

3. Girl Scout activities can be found in books. Girl Scout activities can be found on the Internet. (or)

   _____

4. Our troop visited a blacksmith. Our troop visited a veterinarian. (and)

   _____

5. Do you want to teach art? Do you want to teach physical education? (or)

   _____

6. Find art supplies in the locker. Find art supplies in the cabinet. (or)

   _____

7. Will the girls eat the cookies first? Will the girls eat the brownies first? (or)

   _____

8. Girl Scouts are enthusiastic. Their leaders are enthusiastic. (and)

   _____

9. The bake sale begins Friday. The clothes drive begins Friday. (and)

   _____

10. Join the Girl Scouts for fun. Join the Girl Scouts for adventure. (and)

   _____

At Home: Underline the combined nouns in your written sentences.

27

McGraw-Hill Language Arts
Grade 4, Unit 2, Nouns,
pages 106–107   10

McGraw-Hill School Division

Mechanics and Usage: Abbreviations

> **REMEMBER** THE **RULES**
> - An abbreviation is the shortened form of a word.
> - Abbreviations are used for days, months, addresses, and titles with names.
>
> *Fri., Oct. 1*   *30 River St.*   *Ms. Lucia Potts*   *Sen. John Casey*

A. Write the correct abbreviation next to each word.

1. President _____   6. April _____

2 Thursday _____   7. August _____

3. Street _____   8. Mister _____

4. Wednesday _____   9. Avenue _____

5. February _____   10. November _____

B. Rewrite each sentence using an abbreviation in place of the underlined words.

11. <u>Mister</u> Brooks and Miss Fazio chose new books for our library.

_____

12. Our school is located at 3201 North Vermont <u>Avenue</u>.

_____

13. <u>Doctor</u> Parsen is our school superintendent.

_____

14. Our art class will study the architecture on Main <u>Street</u>.

_____

15. <u>Senator</u> Tom Patton will talk to us about the last election.

_____

15 **McGraw-Hill Language Arts**
Grade 4, Unit 2, Nouns,
pages 108–109

At Home: Write five sentences using abbreviations from Part A.

28

Mixed Review

A. Rewrite each phrase using a possessive noun.

1. the zoo of the children _____

2. the mane of the lion _____

3. the tail of the monkey _____

4. the trunks of the elephants _____

5. the stripes of the tigers _____

B. Write each pair of sentences as one sentence.

6. The lions roar. The tigers roar.

_____

7. Miko saw the monkeys. Miko saw the elephants.

_____

8. Did the nature club go to the zoo? Did the nature club go to the aquarium?

_____

9. The bats are nocturnal. The owls are nocturnal.

_____

10. Dan fed the geese. Dan fed the ducks.

_____

At Home: Ask family members to name their favorite kinds of animal. Then write a sentence about each animal that includes a possessive noun.

McGraw-Hill Language Arts
Grade 4, Unit 2, Mixed Review,
pages 110–111   /10

Common Errors: Plurals and Possessives

REMEMBER THE **RULES**

A **possessive noun** shows who or what owns or has something.

- To form a possessive of a singular noun, add an **-'s.**

    A **zebra's** stripes protect it from other animals.

- To form a possessive of a plural noun that ends in **-s,** add an '.

    The **monkeys'** tails help them keep their balance.

- To form the possessive of a plural noun that does not end in **-s,** add an **-'s.**

    The **geese's** feathers keep them warm in winter.

A. Read each group of words. Label the underlined word *plural, singular possessive,* or *plural possessive.*

1. the <u>lion's</u> den _____

2. the <u>geese's</u> pond _____

3. the <u>birds</u> sing _____

4. the <u>horses'</u> stalls _____

5. the <u>camel's</u> hump _____

B. Rewrite each sentence. Change the underlined words to a singular possessive noun or a plural possessive noun. Add apostrophes correctly.

6. The <u>claws of a lion</u> were very long and sharp.

    _____

7. The <u>howling of wolves</u> kept me awake.

    _____

8. The <u>pond belonging to the geese</u> froze over last winter.

    _____

9. The <u>roars of lions</u> send chills up your spine.

    _____

10. The <u>quills of porcupines</u> struck their mark.

    _____

At Home: Choose three objects in your home. Write a sentence about each one. Include a possessive noun in each sentence.

Study Skills: Parts of a Book

These are important part of books.
- A **title page** shows the title, author, and publisher of a book.
- A **copyright page** shows the date a book was published.
- A **table of contents** lists chapter titles with a beginning page number.
- An **index** lists topics alphabetically with page numbers.
- A **glossary** lists vocabulary words with pronunciations and definitions.

A. Tell which part of the book you would use to find the following information:

1. the page number for the beginning of a chapter entitled "The Aztec Empire"

_____

2. the year in which a book was first published

_____

3. the pronunciation of the term *Conquistadores*

_____

4. the location of the book publisher

_____

5. the page numbers that feature information on the Toltec people

_____

B. Use a nonfiction book to answer each question.

6. What is the name of the publishing company?

_____

7. What is the title and page number for the first chapter?

_____

8. In what year was the book published?

_____

9. What is the second entry in the index?

_____

10. Which word in the glossary interests you most? Write it and its meaning.

_____

At Home: Examine a nonfiction book you have at home. Look at the index. Find a topic of interest and read about it.

McGraw-Hill Language Arts
Grade 4, Unit 2, Study Skills,
pages 120–121

31

/10

McGraw-Hill School Division

Vocabulary: Compound Words

> - A **compound word** is made up of two or more short words joined together.
>
>   *birth* + *day* = birthday
>   *pass* + *word* = password
>   *light* + *house* = lighthouse

Draw lines from words in Column **A** to words in Column **B** to form compound words. Then write the compound word on the lines.

A.	**B.**	
1. bath	brush	_____
2. blood	way	_____
3. hair	house	_____
4. drive	hound	_____
5. club	tub	_____
6. draw	bean	_____
7. law	pan	_____
8. jelly	bridge	_____
9. lady	maker	_____
10. dust	bug	_____
11. finger	ball	_____
12. moon	drop	_____
13. base	print	_____
14. team	mate	_____
15. rain	light	_____

15
McGraw-Hill Language Arts
Grade 4, Unit 2, Vocabulary,
pages 122–123

At Home: Look in the dictionary for six other compound words and use each one in a sentence.

32

Composition Skills: Writing Descriptions

- A **description** creates a clear and vivid picture of a person, place, or thing.
- A good description makes the reader feel as if he or she is actually there.
- Include a sentence that gives a general idea, or overall impression, of the person, place, or thing you are describing.
- Use vivid specific details to tell more about the overall idea.
- Use words that appeal to the senses: sound, sight, smell, touch, and taste.

A. Underline the words in each sentence that create a vivid description.

1. The butterfly had a spot on its wing that looked like splattered ink.

2. The moth fluttered wildly around the light bulb.

3. Doesn't this soup have a spicy aroma?

4. Darma stroked the cat's warm, silky fur.

5. The lion let out a thunderous roar.

B. Complete each sentence with a vivid description of one or more words.

6. My legs moved as fast as _____.

7. I pulled the _____ sweater over my head.

8. Her voice _____ down the hall.

9. The burnt toast left a _____ smell in the room.

10. Does your beverage have a _____ taste?

At Home: Write a paragraph that describe your favorite animal. Use vivid details that appeal to the senses.

McGraw-Hill Language Arts
Grade 4, Unit 2, Composition Skills,
pages 124–125

33

McGraw-Hill School Division

Name_____ Date_____ **Practice** 33a

Features of Writing That Compares

A good example of writing that compares
- explains how two things are **similar.**
- explains how two things are **different.**
- uses **comparison and contrast words** to point out similarities and differences.

A. Read the paragraph. Then, on each side of the Venn Diagram title, write the names of the two topics that are being compared and contrasted.

Linda's two favorite sports are archery and baseball. For archery, she uses a bow and arrow as equipment. For baseball, she uses a ball, bat, and mitt. She does archery by herself, but she plays baseball with a team. She does well in both sports because she has good eye-hand coordination. She does well in baseball because she can run fast. In archery, she is a state champion because she has a very steady hand on the bow and arrow.

1. _____ and 2. _____

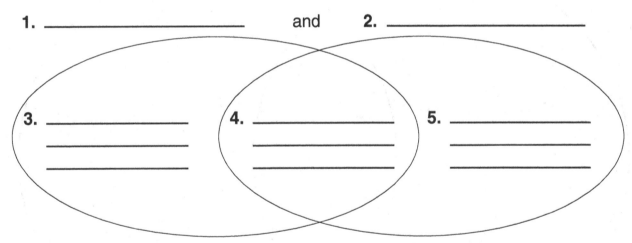

3. _____   4. _____   5. _____

B. Use the information from the paragraph to answer the questions and complete the Venn diagram. Write your answer for each question in the numbered space on the diagram.

3. What is something true about archery that is not true about baseball?

_____

4. What is something true about baseball and archery?

_____

5. What is something about baseball that is not true about archery?

_____

At Home: Think of two sports or activities that you can compare and contrast. Create your own Venn diagram that shows how they are alike and different.

33a

McGraw-Hill School Division

Prewrite: Writing That Compares

Writing that compares describes how two things are alike and how they are different. When you write a comparison, you need to classify your details into two groups. One group should tell how the items are alike, and the other group should list how they are different. You can use a **chart** or **diagram** to compare information.

Think of two things that you want to compare. Then fill in this compare-and-contrast diagram. You can show ways in which the things you compare are alike and different.

Compare-and-Contrast Chart

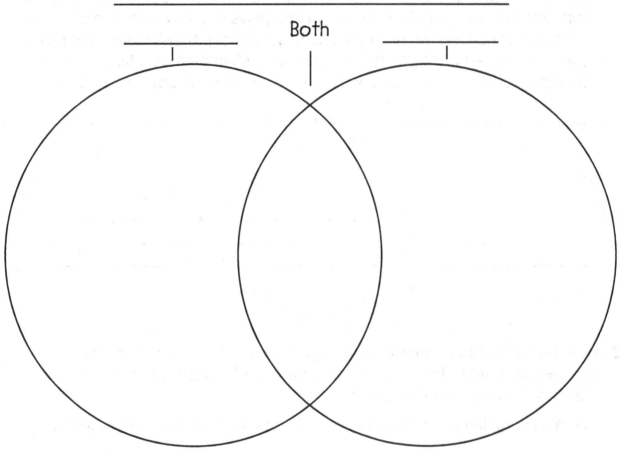

Both

CHECKLIST

• Did you choose things that are both alike and different?

• Have you listed details about each one?

• Can you use those details to compare and contrast?

At Home: Use a chart like the one above to compare and contrast two rooms in your school.

McGraw-Hill Language Arts
Grade 4, Unit 2, Writing That Compares,
pages 134–137

McGraw-Hill School Division

Revise: Writing That Compares

Elaborating can help improve your writing. Adding details to your comparison will make it clearer and more interesting to read.

Read the comparison of the hammerhead shark and the swordfish. Add more details to make the comparison clearer and more interesting. Use the detail box.

Both fish swim in warm waters.
The hammerhead has an eye and a nostril on each side of its head.
The swordfish's sword has two very sharp edges.
Both fish are fast swimmers.

The hammerhead shark and the swordfish are two interesting fish.

Both fish can grow to 15 feet long. Both fish can be a danger to swimmers.

These fish have very different ways of protecting themselves. The

hammerhead has a head shaped like a hammer. Scientists think the

shape of the head helps the shark to move better in the water. Some

scientists also think that its nostrils help the fish to "smell" its prey.

The hammerhead's sharp teeth help it eat fish, including skates and

other sharks.

A swordfish has a jaw that is shaped like a big flat sword. The adult

swordfish doesn't have teeth, but it doesn't need them.

B. Use the changes you marked to rewrite the comparisons on another
piece of paper.

McGraw-Hill Language Arts
Grade 4, Unit 2, Writing That Compares,
pages 140–141

At Home: Look up information about the hammerhead
shark and the swordfish in an encyclopedia. Add two more
details to the comparison above.

33c

Proofread: Writing that Compares

PROOFREADING MARKS	
⌗	new paragraph
∧	add
℘	take out
=	Make a capital letter.
/	Make a small letter.
ⓢⓟ	Check the spelling.
⊙	Add a period.

After you revise your comparison, you will need to **proofread** it to correct any errors.

- Read for correct capitalization and punctuation.
- Read for spelling errors.
- Make sure every sentence has a subject and a predicate.
- Check to be sure plurals have been formed correctly.
- Indent each paragraph.

A. Read the following comparison. Use the proofreading marks from the box to mark any errors you find.

My report is about two kinds of starfish. One is called the crown-of-thorns.

The other is called brittle star. Like most starfish, the brittle star has five arm,

but the crown-of-thorns has 12 to 19 arms. The brittle star can be many

different colors the crown-of-thorns is mostly a reddish color. The crown-of-

thorns can be found on the great Barrier Reef in australia and also in

southern parts of the pacific Ocean. It eats mostly corral. The brittle star has

been found on coastlines from Massachusetts to Brazil. it eats mostly

plankton and it can eat small animals, too.

B. Use the corrections you marked to rewrite the comparison on another piece of paper.

At Home: Write the names of some other marine animals. Think of some ways they are alike and different.

33d

McGraw-Hill Language Arts
Grade 4, Unit 2, Writing That Compares, pages 144–145

10

Action Verbs

┌─ **REMEMBER** THE **RULES** ═══════════════════════════════

- An **action verb** is a word that expresses action. It tells what the subject does or did.

  Joey *joined* the school band.

A. Circle the action verb in each sentence.

1. Joey plays a trumpet in the school band.

2. He takes music lessons once a week.

3. The band practices after school and on weekends.

4. The band marches at the football games.

5. It always performs a halftime show.

6. Band members work hard on each show.

7. The fans cheer the band onto the field.

8. They applaud loudly after each number.

9. The band helps the team's spirit.

10. The fans encourage the band every season.

B. Fill in each blank with an action verb of your own.

11. Joey's family always _____ where they can see the band.

12. They _____ when the band comes onto the field.

13. Sometimes they _____ along with the music.

14. Joey's mother _____ pictures of the action.

15. The spectators _____ during intermission.

|15| **McGraw-Hill Language Arts**
Grade 4, Unit 3, Verbs,
pages 170–171

At Home: Look for an interesting article in a magazine or newspaper. Read the first paragraph. List the action verbs you find.

34

Verb Tenses

- A verb in the **present tense** shows an action that happens now.

   *Marco **collects** insects.*

- A verb in the **past tense** shows an action that has already happened.

   *Marco **collected** insects yesterday.*

- A verb in the **future tense** shows an action that will happen. The special verb **will** is used to form the future tense of verbs.

   *Marco **will collect** another insect tomorrow.*

A. Write *present, past,* or *future* to tell the tense of the underlined verb.

1. Marco <u>studies</u> insects whenever he can. _____

2. He <u>thinks</u> they are fascinating creatures. _____

3. He <u>started</u> studying them several years ago. _____

4. He <u>wanted</u> to become an expert on the subject. _____

5. Many people <u>consider</u> Marco an expert already. _____

6. Marco <u>says</u> insects are the largest group of animals. _____

7. It <u>will take</u> him many years to learn about them. _____

8. Yesterday he <u>talked</u> about them in science class. _____

9. Everyone <u>learned</u> a lot of interesting facts. _____

10. Someday Marco <u>will write</u> his own book

    about insects. _____

B. Underline the verb in each sentence. Then write *present, past,* or *future* to tell the tense of the verb.

11. Scientists named about 800,000 kinds of insects. _____

12. They classify about 7,000 new kinds every year. _____

13. Insects live almost everywhere on earth. _____

14. Scientists will discover many more kinds in the future. _____

15. Maybe Marco will help them. _____

At Home: Read an article in a magazine or newspaper. Find two examples each of present-tense, past-tense, and future-tense verbs.

McGraw-Hill Language Arts
Grade 4, Unit 3, Verbs,
pages 172–173

35

/15

McGraw-Hill School Division

Name_____ Date_____ **Practice** 36

Subject-Verb Agreement

┌─ **REMEMBER** THE **RULES** ─────────────────────
│ • The subject and verb in a sentence must **agree.**
│ • Add **-s** to most present-tense verbs if the subject is singular.
│   *Our **camera takes** great pictures.*
│ • Add **-es** to present-tense verbs that end in *s, ch, sh, x,* or *z.*
│   *My **sister searches** for things to photograph.*
│ • Do not add **-s** or **-es** if the subject is plural or if it is *I* or *you.*
│   ***Computers send** photos over the Internet.*
└──

A. Circle the present-tense verb form that agrees with the subject in dark type.

1. **Carla and Mario** (like, likes) to take photographs.

2. **Mario** (photograph, photographs) things in nature.

3. **I** (look, looks) for unusual situations to photograph.

4. **Mario** (fuss, fusses) over every shot he takes.

5. **Carla** (take, takes) photographs of people and pets.

B. Write each sentence. Use the correct form of the verb in parentheses ( ).

6. Many people (enjoy) taking pictures.

_____

7. You (capture) special moments in time.

_____

8. Carla (send) photographs with her computer.

_____

9. She (share) stories of her travels in her letters.

_____

10. Carla (reach) many of her friends this way.

_____

McGraw-Hill Language Arts
Grade 4, Unit 3, Verbs,
pages 174–175

At Home: Read a paragraph from a favorite book. Tell if the subject of each sentence is singular or plural.

36

Spelling Present-Tense and Past-Tense Verbs

> **REMEMBER** THE **RULES**
>
> • **Change the *y* to *i*** before adding *-es* or *-ed* to verbs that end with a consonant and *y.*
>
>   *Mark **hurries** to mail a package.   Mark **hurried** to mail a package.*
>
> • **Double the final consonant** before adding *-ed* to one-syllable verbs that end in one vowel and one consonant.
>
>   *He **wrapped** the package carefully.   He **moved** quickly to get there.*
>
> • **Drop the *e*** before adding *-ed* to verbs that end in *e.*

A. Write the correct present- and past-tense form of each verb in parentheses.

1. Miko _____ some delicate rice paper. (purchase)

2. She _____ on several colors of ink.(decide)

3. She also _____ out several kinds of pens. (try)

4. Finally, Miko _____ home to begin a drawing. (hurry)

5. Miko's brother _____ when he saw her work. (clap)

B. Look at the tense shown after each sentence. Then write each sentence using the correct form of the verb in parentheses.

6. Miko always (try) to do her best. *present*

_____

7. Sometimes she (copy) something over to get it right. *present*

_____

8. Once she (worry) that she had spoiled a picture. *past*

_____

9. Her parents (notice) that she was a good artist. *past*

_____

10 They (hope) she would keep trying. *past*

_____

McGraw-Hill School Division

Mechanics and Usage: Commas in a Series

> **REMEMBER** THE **RULES**
> • Use **commas** to separate three or more words in a series.
> • Do not use a comma after the last word in a series.
>   *Friends are kind, considerate, and respectful of each other.*

A. Add commas where they are needed in each sentence.

1. David Jesse and Sara are best friends.

2. They like to work play and study together.

3. David enjoys drawing painting and sketching.

4. Jesse likes to play soccer baseball basketball and hockey.

5. Sara likes to write poetry stories and plays.

6. The three friends enjoy hiking swimming and jogging together.

7. They often talk about sports music movies and their favorite TV shows.

8. Sometimes they go to movies concerts or plays together.

9. They often write e-mail or fax one another.

10. The three friends are kind loyal and honest with one another.

B. Write each sentence. Add commas where they are needed. Take them out where they are not needed.

11. Marge, Megen and Mike, made a poster about recycling.

_____

12. They used cardboard markers colored paper and paints to make it.

_____

13. Recycling, of paper metal and glass is the theme of the poster.

_____

14. Their teachers thought the poster was clever, thoughtful, and, well-made.

_____

15. The message was clear accurate and important.

_____

McGraw-Hill Language Arts
Grade 4, Unit 3, Verbs,
pages 178–179
15

At Home: Write five sentences about your neighborhood to show how commas are used after words in a series.

38

Mixed Review

REMEMBER THE **RULES**

- A verb in the **present tense** shows an action that is happening now.
- A verb in the **past tense** shows an action that has already happened.
- A verb in the **future tense** shows an action that will happen.
- Add *-s* to most present-tense verbs if the subject is singular. Add *-es* to verbs that end in *s, ch, sh, x,* or *z.* Do not add *-s* or *-es* if the subject is plural or *I* or *you.*
- For verbs ending in a consonant and *y,* change the *y* to *i* before adding *-es* or *-ed.*
- For one-syllable verbs ending in one vowel and one consonant, double the consonant before adding *-ed.*
- For verbs ending in *e,* drop the *e* before adding *-ed.*

A. Look at the tense shown after each sentence. Then write the correct form of the verb in parentheses.

1. People (share) information in different ways. (present) _____

2. Sometimes they (write) letters to friends. (present) _____

3. Yesterday, I (use) my computer to send information. (past) _____

4. This morning, I (talk) to several people. (past) _____

5. I (call) my parents to tell them where I was. (past) _____

6. Someday, we (wear) phones on our wrists. (future) _____

7. My uncle (buy) a cellular phone next week. (future) _____

8. Television (send) information to everyone. (present) _____

9. This morning, I (listen) to the radio for news. (past) _____

10. Someday, I (make) a movie to share my ideas. (future) _____

At Home: Think about ways you communicate with your family and friends. Describe the ways in a paragraph. Include verbs in the present, past, and future tense.

39

McGraw-Hill Language Arts
Grade 4, Unit 3, Mixed Review,
pages 180–181

/10

McGraw-Hill School Division

Main Verbs and Helping Verbs

> **REMEMBER** THE **RULES**
> - The **main verb** in a sentence tells what the subject does or is.
> - A **helping verb** helps the main verb show an action or make a statement.
>
>   *Mike's class **is planning** a talent show.*
>
>   ↑   ↑
>   **helping main**
>   **verb   verb**

A. Underline each helping verb. Circle each main verb.

1. Our class has decided to have a talent show.

2. It will take a lot of planning.

3. Everyone will need to get involved.

4. Some students are working on announcements.

5. Others were designing the program brochure.

6. Several students are working to set up the auditorium.

7. One person was adjusting the stage lighting.

8. Several people are building props and sets.

9. I am helping on the talent committee.

10. We will find many talented performers.

B. Write a helping verb for each main verb.

11. Today our entire class _____ excited about the talent show.

12. Yesterday some people _____ practicing musical numbers.

13. One group _____ present a gymnastic routine.

14. Soon one person _____ going to put on a magic show.

15. Now several people _____ playing musical instruments.

McGraw-Hill Language Arts
Grade 4, Unit 3, Verbs,
15 **pages 182–183**

At Home: Write four sentences to describe a talent you have or would like to have. Include a helping verb and main verb in each sentence.

Using Helping Verbs

┌─ **REMEMBER** THE **RULES** ═══════════════════════════

- Use the **helping verbs *has, have,*** and ***had*** with the past-tense form of a verb to show an action that has already happened.

  *Jill **has decided** to visit the aquarium.*

  *I **had decided** to go last week.*

  *We **have decided** to go together.*

A. Circle the correct form of the helping verb in parentheses.

1. I (have, has) visited the aquarium many times before.

2. Jill (have, had) traveled there once, but it was closed.

3. We (has, had) planned to go together for some time.

4. Now we (has, have) promised to go with each other.

5. We (have, has) decided to visit the coral reef exhibit first.

6. The exhibit (have, has) attracted the most visitors.

7. The sharks (has, have) added to its popularity since I was there.

8. Sharks (have, has) interested me for a long time.

9. I (has, had) witnessed the sharks being fed once before.

10. I thought the divers (has, had) displayed a lot of bravery.

B. Complete each sentence. Use *has, have,* or *had* and the correct form of the verb in parentheses.

11. The aquarium _____ animal acts for years. (include)

12. By the time we got there, the seals _____ twice. (bark)

13. Now the porpoises _____ over three buoys. (jump)

14. They _____ remarkable feats in their show. (perform)

15. The show _____ people understand the intelligence of animals. (help)

At Home: Write three sentences about something that has happened to you. Use the helping verbs *have, has,* or *had* in each sentence.

McGraw-Hill Language Arts
Grade 4, Unit 3, Verbs,
pages 184–185

15

McGraw-Hill School Division

Linking Verbs

┌─ **REMEMBER** THE **RULES** ──────────────────────────────────
│
│ • A **linking verb** links the subject of a sentence to a noun or adjective in
│   the predicate.
│
│ • A linking verb does not show action.
│   *Koalas **are** animals from Australia.*
│
│ • The words *am, is, are, was*, and *were* are frequently used as
│   linking verbs.
│
└──

A. Decide if the underlined verb is a linking verb or an action verb.
Circle your answer.

1. I <u>am</u> a great koala fan.   **action verb   linking verb**

2. I often <u>visit</u> them at my local zoo.   **action verb   linking verb**

3. These animals <u>remind</u> people of teddy bears. **action verb   linking verb**

4. A koala <u>is</u> really a relative of the kangaroo. **action verb   linking verb**

5. A koala mother <u>carries</u> her babies in a pouch. **action verb   linking verb**

6. Koalas <u>spend</u> most of their time in trees.   **action verb   linking verb**

7. Their claws <u>are</u> long and sharp for climbing.   **action verb   linking verb**

8. A koala <u>is</u> a creature of the night.   **action verb   linking verb**

9. They <u>sleep</u> most of the day.   **action verb   linking verb**

10. Koalas <u>are</u> protected by Australian laws.   **action verb   linking verb**

B. Underline the verb in each sentence. Write *linking* or *action* to tell
what kind of verb it is.

11. Koalas eat mainly the leaves of eucalyptus trees. _____

12. Koala fur is soft and thick. _____

13. Koalas are from 25 to 30 inches long. _____

14. They weigh from 15 to 30 pounds. _____

15. The koalas are favorites at my zoo. _____

15 | **McGraw-Hill Language Arts**
Grade 4, Unit 3, Verbs,
pages 186–187

At Home: Write a riddle using linking verbs. See if a friend
or relative can solve it.

42

Using Linking Verbs

> **REMEMBER** THE **RULES**
>
> - A **linking verb** is a verb that links the subject of a sentence with an adjective or noun in the predicate.
>
>   *Adam **is** in my class.*
>
> - A **linking verb** must agree with the subject.
> - Different forms of the verb **be** are most often used as linking verbs.
>
>   *Yesterday **was** Adam's big day.*

A. Draw a circle around the linking verb in each sentence.

1. Adam is editor of the class newsletter.

2. Several of his classmates are reporters.

3. They are also writers of several of the articles.

4. One person is an artist for the newsletter.

5. It was a difficult job putting out the first issue.

6. The first issue was a wonderful surprise.

7. Everyone thought it was a huge success.

8. "It is one of the best we have ever had," Adam's teacher said.

9. "I am glad we have one of our own," said a friend.

10. Adam and his staff were a happy group.

B. Complete each sentence with a linking verb from the box.

am	is	are	was	were

11. Two years ago, David _____ a beginning magician.

12. His shows _____ always on Saturdays.

13. A floating ball _____ a prop for one popular trick.

14. I _____ one of his devoted fans.

15. His friends _____ surprised by his talent.

At Home: Read a page from a favorite book. List all the linking verbs you find.

McGraw-Hill Language Arts
Grade 4, Unit 3, Verbs,
pages 188–189

43

15

McGraw-Hill School Division

Irregular Verbs

┌─ **REMEMBER** THE **RULES** ═══════════════════════

- **Irregular verbs** are verbs that do not add *–ed* to form the past tense. Instead, the spelling of the verb changes.

    *I **go** to park concerts.*

    *I **went** to a park concert*

    *I **have gone** to park concerts.*

A. Circle the correct past-tense form of the verb in parentheses.

1. Midge (see, saw) a poster at the city pool.

2. We had (swam, swum) there several times before.

3. She (run, ran) over to read the poster.

4. The poster (gave, given) information about a park concert.

5. She and I (make, made) plans to go to the concert.

B. Write each sentence. Use the correct past-tense form of the verb in parentheses.

6. The audience (sing) along to some of the songs.

_____

7. The performers had (give) a great show.

_____

8. The applause (bring) everyone to their feet.

_____

9. Midge and I (run) up to the stage at the end.

_____

10. The performers had (go) by the time we got there.

_____

[10] **McGraw-Hill Language Arts**
Grade 4, Unit 3, Verbs,
pages 190–191

At Home: Look through a magazine article to find
examples of sentences written in the past tense.

44

More Irregular Verbs

REMEMBER THE **RULES**

- **Irregular verbs** do not add *–ed* to form the past tense. They usually change their spelling.

    I **wrote** a letter to my pen pal.

- The past form of an **irregular verb** changes when used with *has*, *have*, or *had*.

    I **have written** to my pen pal many times.

A. Circle the irregular verb in each sentence.

1. We had grown up together.

2. We had begun writing because he moved.

3. Sometimes I have drawn pictures to send him.

4. Last year, he flew to visit me.

5. I threw him a surprise party the next day.

6. We swam in the city pool several times.

7. We rode horses at my grandfather's farm.

8. I had ridden many times before.

9. It took my friend a little time to catch on.

10. My parents also drove us to the county fair.

B. Complete each sentence with the correct form of an irregular verb.

11. Yoshi has _____ some beautiful pictures.

12. He _____ drawing when he was very little.

13. Our local newspaper has _____ an article about him.

14. They also _____ a photograph of him working.

15. Then they _____ a party for him.

At Home: Write three sentences about a place you visited. Use irregular verbs in the past tense in each sentence.

McGraw-Hill Language Arts
Grade 4, Unit 3, Verbs,
pages 192–193

45

/15

Mechanics and Usage: Contractions with *Not*

REMEMBER THE **RULES**

- A **contraction** is a shortened form of two words.
- An **apostrophe** (') takes the place of one or more letters.

    We **did not** watch television last night.

    We **didn't** watch television last night.

A. Write the contraction for each of the following pairs of words.

1. has not _____

2. will not _____

3. is not _____

4. are not _____

5. were not _____

6. did not _____

7. have not _____

8. do not _____

9. was not _____

10. does not _____

B. Write each sentence using a contraction for the underlined words.

11. I <u>do not</u> watch much television anymore.

_____

12. The shows <u>have not</u> been very interesting.

_____

13. I <u>was not</u> able to find anything worth watching last night.

_____

14. When the shows <u>are not</u> interesting, I read.

_____

15. It <u>does not</u> hurt to read a good book.

_____

McGraw-Hill Language Arts
Grade 4, Unit 3, Verbs,
pages 194–195

15

At Home: List as many contractions as you can. Then
choose five and write them in sentences.

Mixed Review

> **REMEMBER** THE **RULES**
>
> - The **main verb** in a sentence shows what a subject does or is.
>   *Kim **paints** pictures on pieces of wood.*
> - A **helping verb** helps the main verb show an action or make a statement.
>   *He **has** won some prizes at crafts fairs.*
> - A **linking verb** connects the subject to a noun or adjective in the predicate. A linking verb does not show action.
>   *He **is** a talented artist.*

A. Draw one line under each main verb. Draw two lines under each helping verb. Circle each linking verb.

1. David and I have lived near each other for many years.

2. He has received many awards for his art work.

3. This morning, he was working in his studio.

4. David had made a sketch early in the week.

5. The sketch is a picture of a local landscape.

B. Write each sentence. Use the correct form of the verb in parentheses ( ).

6. David's father (have, has) painted for many years

   _____

7. Some of his paintings (is, are) hanging in museums.

   _____

8. I have never (seen, saw) such beautiful work.

   _____

9. He (have, has) painted many scenes with the sea as the subject.

   _____

10. We (was, were) happy to see him become so successful.

   _____

At Home: Think of something you do well. Describe it in a paragraph. Include some helping and linking verbs in your sentences.

47

McGraw-Hill Language Arts
Grade 4, Unit 3, Mixed Review,
pages 196–197   /10

McGraw-Hill School Division

Common Errors: Subject-Verb Agreement

┌───┐
REMEMBER THE **RULES**

- When the parts of a compound subject are joined by **and,** use a plural verb.

  *A whale **and** a dolphin **swim** side-by-side.*

- When the parts of a compound subject are joined by **or,** the verb agrees with the subject that is closer to it.

  *A whale **or** dolphins often **come** up to the side of the boat.*

- **Remember:** When a verb ends with a consonant and **y,** change the **y** to **i** and add **-es** to form a singular verb. *cry → cries*

- **Remember:** When a verb ends with a vowel and **y,** add **-s** to form a singular verb. Do not change the spelling of the verb. *pays → pays*
└───┘

A. Write the correct form of the underlined verb.

1. Whales and dolphins <u>is</u> mammals, not fish. _____

2. Kim and I <u>goes</u> whale watching whenever we can. _____

3. Tourists and locals <u>enjoys</u> watching the whales. _____

4. The captain and crew <u>seems</u> to know exactly where to go. _____

5. The wind or current <u>carry</u> the ship to its destination. _____

B. Write the correct form of the verb in parentheses ( ).

6. Blue whales and fin whales (get) to be over 80 feet long. _____

7. A beluga or a narwhal (grow) only 10 to 15 feet long. _____

8. Fin whales and Minke whales (feed) on small fish. _____

9. Flippers and flukes (help) whales to swim. _____

10. Some laws (protect) most kinds of whales. _____

McGraw-Hill Language Arts
Grade 4, Unit 3, Verbs
pages 198–199
10

At Home: Write three sentences about a trip you have taken. Include a compound subject in each sentence.

48

Study Skills: Card Catalog

- Every library book is listed in the **card catalog** of a library. You can search by **author, title,** or **subject** to find a book.
- The card catalog is in a set of drawers or on a computer.
- Each kind of card shows the same information in a different order.
- All cards are arranged in alphabetical order.
- All cards have call numbers that help you locate the book in the library.

A. Use the subject card below to answer the questions.

```
624        BRIDGES
S
        St. George, Judith
    The Brooklyn Bridge: They Said
        It Couldn't Be Built.
New York: G. P. Putnam's Sons, © 1982.
125 p.: illus.
ISBN 0-399-61282-3
```

1. What is the title of the book?

   _____

2. Who is the author? _____

3. When was the book published? _____

4. What is the call number of the book? _____

5. How many pages are in the book? _____

B. Tell whether you would use an **author card, title card,** or **subject card** to answer each question.

6. Who wrote *A Wrinkle in Time?* _____

7. What are titles of books written by E. B. White? _____

8. What book will help me learn about the rules of soccer? _____

9. Is there a biography of Jacqueline Kennedy Onassis? _____

10. How many books by Louis Sachar does the library have?

    _____

At Home: Write another question that could be answered by each of the following kinds of cards in the card catalog: **49** author card, subject card, title card.

McGraw-Hill Language Arts **Grade 4, Unit 3, Study Skills, pages 206–207** /10

Vocabulary: Prefixes

> • A **prefix** is a word part added to the beginning of a base word that changes the meaning of the base word.
>
> **disagree:** *I disagree with you. I do not agree with you.*
>
> **rewind:** *Please rewind the tape. Please wind the tape again.*

A. Circle each word that has a prefix. Write it in the box.

Mom had prearranged an appointment with the dentist for me. Now she has to reschedule it. I reminded her about my signing up for soccer just at that time. She apologized and said she had misunderstood me. She said that my calendar is so full, she is incapable of keeping track of where I should be.

1. _____
2. _____
3. _____
4. _____
5. _____

B. Add a prefix to a base word to replace the underlined words. Write the new sentence on the line.

6. Half of my math answers were <u>not correct</u>.

_____

7. I am <u>not capable</u> of understanding fractions.

_____

8. I have to <u>do</u> five problems <u>again</u>.

_____

9. My teacher is never <u>not patient</u> with me.

_____

10. Do you agree that it's <u>not possible</u> to subtract 15 from $3\frac{1}{2}$?

_____

McGraw-Hill Language Arts
Grade 4, Unit 3, Vocabulary, pages 208–209
10

At Home: List three other words for each of these prefixes: *pre-*, *im-*, and *mis-*.

50

Composition Skills: Leads and Endings

- A **lead** is the first part of something written. It should capture a reader's attention.
- You may state your **main idea** in the lead.
- An **ending** is the last part of something written.
- Write a good ending to give your reader a feeling of closure, or completeness.

A. Read each pair of leads or endings. Then underline the one that is stronger.

1. Danny walks dogs as part of a dog-walking service.

   Name the time, and Danny will be your dog walker.

2. Tomorrow we will have a car wash.

   Picture this: a newly washed car gleaming like the sun.

3. Test your ability to persuade by joining the debate club today.

   You can join the debate club if you would like to.

4. Be ready for an unimaginable adventure when you open *The Time Slide*.

   The book *The Time Slide* tells an adventure story that also entertains readers.

5. Come one, come all to a class picnic on Thursday evening.

   There is a class picnic that will take place on Thursday evening.

B. Read each topic. Then, write a strong lead sentence.

6. A favorite book _____

   _____

7. A school soccer team _____

   _____

8. A Science Fair _____

   _____

9. Student volunteers _____

   _____

10. First Day in a New School _____

   _____

At Home: Choose a piece of persuasive writing that you have already written. Now, write a stronger lead or a stronger ending.

McGraw-Hill Language Arts
Grade 4, Unit 3, Composition Skills,
pages 210–211 / 10

Features of Persuasive Writing

Good persuasive writing
- clearly states the **author's opinion** on a topic.
- supports the opinion with **convincing reasons** and arguments.
- organizes reasons in a **logical order.**
- often saves the **strongest reasons** for last.
- includes **opinion words.**

A. Read the paragraph. Underline the author's clearly-stated opinion.

1. What should be done with the empty lot next to our school? The best use for the empty lot, I think, would be to plant and maintain a garden. If students could help take care of the garden, they would experience interesting hands-on science lessons about plant life. In addition, students would learn valuable social-studies lessons about helping out in the community. Most of all, an unpleasant piece of unused land would turn into a colorful, lively place. No one in our school or community would lose if flowers and plants replaced dust and trash.

B. Use the paragraph to answer the following questions.

2. What phrase in the second sentence shows that the author will state an opinion?

_____

3. What is one strong reason that supports the author's opinion?

_____

4. What is one convincing reason the author uses to support his or her opinion?

_____

_____

5. What is another convincing reason the author uses to support his or her opinion?

_____

_____

McGraw-Hill Language Arts
Grade 4, Unit 3, Persuasive Writing,
pages 218–219
5

At Home: Write a sentence that states your opinion on an issue related to your school or community. List three reasons that support your opinion.

51a

Prewrite: Persuasive Writing

Writing **persuasively** is a good way to share an opinion about something you feel strongly about. You can use both fact and opinion to support your position. Before you write, it is important to understand what exactly is a fact and what is an opinion. A chart can help you keep track of facts and opinions.

Pretend you are a member of a group that has to come up with a topic for a research report. You want to convince others in your group to write about a particular topic. List facts and opinions you can use to convince them.

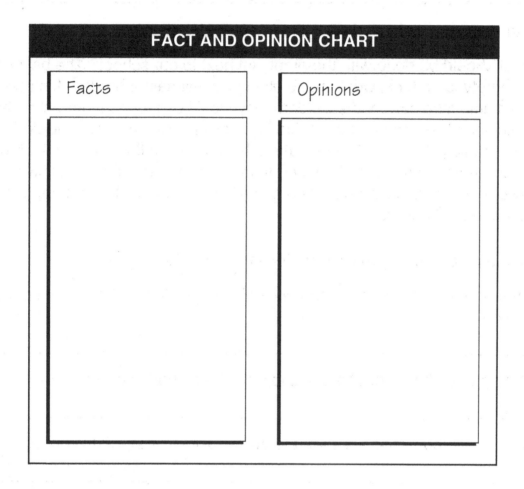

FACT AND OPINION CHART

Facts

Opinions

CHECKLIST

• Did you list enough facts and opinions to convince your group?

• Are your items listed in an organized way?

• Do you need to do more research?

At Home: Write a paragraph to try to convince your real or imaginary brother or sister that you have a right to a later bedtime.

51b

McGraw-Hill Language Arts
Grade 4, Unit 3, Persuasive Writing,
pages 220–221

Revise: Persuasive Writing

You can elaborate your persuasive writing by adding details and choosing words that will convince your readers to agree with your opinions. When you **revise** your work, you need to make your argument stronger, or more persuasive.

A. Pretend you wrote this persuasive writing. Revise it by adding opinion words or phrases. Choose from the word box or use your own. You can also add your own opinions or facts to improve the writing.

believe	exciting	interesting	great
best	wonderful	famous	largest

Let's research how and why the pyramids were built. The Great

Pyramid and is one of the Seven Wonders of the World. It was built as

the tomb of Pharaoh Khufu. It was 480 feet high. Each of its sides was

756 feet wide at the base.

I'm sure you'll want to know how the workers built the pyramids and

why they built them, too. I've done some research and found out that the

Egyptians believed in life after death.

Everybody is always interested in mummies. We can find out what

the Egyptians used to preserve them. We can learn to write some

hieroglyphics, too. We can find pictures of statues of pharaohs and

famous queens. Don't you agree that this is a topic to study?

B. Write the new paragraphs on a separate sheet of paper.

McGraw-Hill Language Arts
Grade 4, Unit 3, Persuasive Writing,
pages 226–227

At Home: Pretend you are an ancient Egyptian child. Write a paragraph to convince your father, the pharaoh, that you are old enough to attend a big ceremony. Use facts and opinions to support your argument. **51c**

Proofread: Persuasive Writing

PROOFREADING MARKS	
⯗	new paragraph
∧	add
ᕼ	take out
═	Make a capital letter.
/	Make a small letter.
ⓢ𝕡	Check the spelling.
⊙	Add a period.

After you have revised your persuasive writing, you will need to **proofread** it to correct any errors.

• Read each sentence to check for correct use of capital letters.

• Check the end of each sentence for proper punctuation.

• Check for errors in grammar.

• Reread for spelling errors.

• Combine sentences to make the writing smoother.

A. Read the following paragraphs from a persuasive book report. Use the proofreading marks from the box to mark any errors you find.

One chapter of this book was about Martin luther king, Jr. If you read this book I know you will agree that he was a very brave man. You should know about how he helps African americans use their civil rights.

Do you know Rosa Parks.   When she refused to give up her seat on a crowded bus so a white person could sit down She was arrested. Dr. King led a boycott. He got people to refuse to rode the bus for 381 days. That boycott was an important point in the civil rights movment.

You just have to read this book

B. On another sheet of paper, use your corrections to rewrite the paragraphs.

At Home: Read a book about Martin Luther King, Jr., or look his name up in an encyclopedia. Find out more about him.

51d

McGraw-Hill Language Arts
Grade 4, Unit 3, Persuasive Writing,
pages 230–231

10

McGraw-Hill School Division

Adjectives

> **REMEMBER** THE **RULES**
> - **Adjectives** are words that describe nouns.
>   *I live in a **friendly** neighborhood.*
> - **Adjectives** can tell *what kind* or *how many.*
>   *There are **three new** families on my street.*

A. Underline the adjective in each sentence. Circle the noun it describes.

1. I live in an interesting neighborhood.

2. Tall trees line the streets.

3. The houses have large lawns.

4. Beautiful gardens are just about everywhere you look.

5. There is an unusual statue across the street.

6. It is a small copy of a pyramid.

7. A special friend of mine lives in an apartment.

8. Her tall building is next to the park.

9. It has a fancy fountain in front of it.

10. During the cold winter the fountain froze.

B. Complete each sentence with an adjective of your own.

11. A large, old _____ tree grows in our yard.

12. My grandfather planted the tree _____ years ago.

13. The tree provides _____ shade for our house.

14. Once during a storm a _____ limb broke off the tree.

15. My grandfather used the wood to build a _____ table.

McGraw-Hill Language Arts
Grade 4, Unit 4, Adjectives,
pages 262–263
15

At Home: Look for an article in a magazine or newspaper that sounds interesting. Read the first paragraph. List the adjectives you find.

Articles: *a, an, the*

> **REMEMBER** THE **RULES**
>
> - *A, an*, and *the* are special adjectives called articles.
> - Use *a* and *an* before singular nouns. Use *a* if the next word begins with a consonant sound. Use *an* if the next word begins with a vowel sound.
>   *Yosemite is **a** national park.   It is **an** interesting place to see.*
> - Use *the* before singular nouns that name a particular person, place, or thing, and before plural nouns.
>   ***The** views are breathtaking.*

A. Circle the article or articles in each sentence.

1. Yosemite National Park is a great wilderness area.

2. It is located in the Sierra Nevada Mountains.

3. There is also a grove of giant redwood trees.

4. The waterfalls are breathtaking during the spring.

5. Bicycling is an interesting way to see the valley.

B. Rewrite each sentence with the correct article.

6. Yosemite is (a, an) year-round park.

_____

7. (The, An) park has more than 60 kinds of animals.

_____

8. You might see (a, an) deer or bear at your cabin door.

_____

9. You might hear (a, an) mountain lion roar in (the, a) night.

_____

10. (A, An) visit to (an, the) park is (a, an) unforgettable experience.

_____

McGraw-Hill School Division

At Home: Read a paragraph from a magazine, newspaper, or favorite book. Count the number of times you see *a, an,* or *the.*

53

McGraw-Hill Language Arts
Grade 4, Unit 4, Adjectives,
pages 264–265

/10

Adjectives After Linking Verbs

REMEMBER THE RULES

- When an **adjective** comes after the noun it describes, the two are connected by a **linking verb.**

  *The sky **was** dark.*   *A storm **is** threatening.*

A. Draw one line under the adjective. Draw two lines under the noun it describes. Circle the linking verb.

1. Hurricanes are strong.

2. A hurricane is dangerous.

3. The winds are powerful.

4. The rain is heavy.

5. During a hurricane, waves are huge.

6. Flooding is serious.

7. Damage from a hurricane is costly.

8. This year the storms were severe.

9. The hurricane was forceful.

10. The damage to homes was unbelievable.

B. Complete each sentence with an adjective that makes sense. Circle the noun the adjective describes.

11. The clouds were _____ with rain.

12. The wind was _____ with tremendous force.

13. The storm is _____ near the shore.

14. The damage from the wind was _____.

15. Storms like this are _____.

At Home: Describe your favorite kind of weather. Use linking verbs and adjectives.

Mechanics and Usage: Proper Adjectives

> **REMEMBER** THE **RULES**
> - **Proper adjectives** are formed from proper nouns.
> - **Proper adjectives** are always capitalized.
>   *I like to eat at **Chinese** restaurants.*

A. Underline each proper adjective. Circle the noun it describes.

1. You have probably eaten many European foods.

2. For example, have you ever tasted Irish stew?

3. The Midwest is known for its German sausages.

4. James likes Canadian bacon.

5. There are also wonderful Mexican foods.

6. Almost everyone has eaten a Chinese meal.

7. America is also known for its foods, like Maine lobster.

8. A favorite at many holiday meals is Virginia ham.

9. Let's not forget New England clam chowder.

10. More good foods can be found in Italian restaurants.

B. Rewrite each sentence. Capitalize each proper adjective.

11. Have you ever eaten a mexican tortilla?

_____

12. Have you ever tried a chinese stir fry?

_____

13. Have you ever made japanese tempura?

_____

14. Have you ever tasted an indian curry?

_____

15. Have you ever ordered italian lasagna?

_____

At Home: Ask family members to name the foods from different countries they like. Write three adjectives to tell about each food. Include a proper adjective.

McGraw-Hill Language Arts
Grade 4, Unit 4, Adjectives,
pages 268–269   /15

McGraw-Hill School Division

Mixed Review

A. Underline each adjective. Circle the noun that the adjective describes.

1. Origami developed as a Japanese art.

2. Experts practice for many years.

3. The paper is folded into decorative objects.

4. Traditional figures make up most of the objects.

5. The Japanese paper used most is called washi.

B. Rewrite each sentence. Capitalize each proper adjective.

6. Have you ever painted a japanese garden?

   _____

7. Have you ever been to the egyptian pyramids?

   _____

8. Have you ever seen native american pottery?

   _____

9. Have you ever been to the galapagos islands?

   _____

10. Have you ever sung an african song?

   _____

10 **McGraw-Hill Language Arts** **Grade 4, Unit 4, Mixed Review,** pages 270–271

At Home: Write about a hobby you or a family member has. When you finish writing, underline the adjectives you used and circle the words they describe.

56

Adjectives That Compare

┌─ **REMEMBER** THE **RULES** ═══════════════════════════

- Add **-er** to most adjectives to compare two people, places, or things.

    *A Maltese has **longer** fur than a Chihuahua.*

- Add **-est** to most adjectives to compare more than two.

    *Pugs are the **largest** of all toy dogs.*

└──

A. Underline the adjective that compares.

1. The Chihuahua is the smallest of all dogs.

2. A Shar Pei has the loosest skin of any dog.

3. Collies have narrower heads than boxers.

4. The Irish wolfhound is the tallest dog in the world.

5. Boxers have shorter hair than German shepherds.

6. German shepherds have straighter hair than poodles.

7. A Kerry blue terrier's coat is softer than a collie's coat.

8. Pekingeses have broader faces than terriers.

9. Terriers are some of the bravest of all dogs.

10. Retrievers are faster swimmers than hounds.

B. Write the correct form of the adjective in parentheses ( ).

11. A dog's sense of smell is the _____ of all its
    senses. (strong)

12. Some people think hounds have the _____ bark of
    any dog. (deep)

13. The terrier group is _____ than the toy group of
    dogs. (large)

14. Dachshunds are _____ than greyhounds. (small)

15. An Irish terrier's coat is _____ than a smooth fox terrier's
    coat. (dark)

At Home: Write five sentences describing a pet you have or
would like to have. Include at least three adjectives that
compare.

McGraw-Hill School Division

Spelling Adjectives That Compare

┌─ **REMEMBER** THE **RULES** ─────────────────────────

- Change a final *y* to *i* before adding *-er* or *-est.*

  *Which state is the **rainiest** of all the states?*

- Drop a final *e* before adding *-er* or *-est.*

  *Is Nevada or Utah **closer** to Mexico?*

- Double the final consonant after a single vowel before adding *-er* or *-est.*

  *Which state is the **hottest** state of all?*

A. Underline the adjective that compares. Write the root word on the line.

1. Rhode Island is the smallest of all the states. _____

2. Alaska is the biggest of all the states. _____

3. North Carolina is hillier than Nebraska. _____

4. Oregon is rainier than New Mexico. _____

5. Hawaii may have the prettiest beaches of all. _____

Rhode Island

B. Rewrite each sentence. Use the correct form of the adjective in parentheses ( ).

6. Alaska is the (wide) of the states.

_____

Alaska

7. Utah is (close) than Nebraska is to the Pacific Ocean.

_____

Utah

8. Iowa may be the (flat) of all the states.

_____

9. New Mexico is probably the (square) of all the states.

_____

New Mexico

10. Nevada is probably the (sandy) state of all.

_____

McGraw-Hill School Division

10 **McGraw-Hill Language Arts**
Grade 4, Unit 4, Adjectives,
pages 274–275

At Home: Read an article from a magazine or newspaper.
Look for adjectives that change their spelling when they
compare. Make a list of the ones you find.

58

Comparing with *More* and *Most*

┌─ **REMEMBER** THE **RULES** ─────────────────────────┐

• Use *more* to compare two people, places, or things.

  I think hiking is **more enjoyable** *than swimming.*

• Use *most* to compare more than two.

  I think hiking is the **most enjoyable** *of all outdoor activities.*

└──────────────────────────────────────┘

A. Complete each sentence with *more* or *most*.

1. The zoo trip was _____ fun than the one to the library.

2. The hiking trip was the _____ interesting trip all year.

3. It was the _____ beautiful day of the summer.

4. This hiking trail was _____ difficult than last year's.

5. Our hike was _____ exciting than last year's, too.

B. Rewrite each sentence. Use the correct form of the adjective in parentheses ( ).

6. The winding trail was (fascinating) than the one we took before.

   _____

   _____

7. The mountains provided the (scenic) view of all.

   _____

8. The view from the top was (impressive) than the view from below.

   _____

   _____

9 The hike down was (interesting) than the hike up.

   _____

10. People were (relaxed) than they were at the beginning.

   _____

At Home: Choose two or three things at home that you can compare. Write comparisons about them using the words *more* and *most*.

59

McGraw-Hill Language Arts
Grade 4, Unit 4, Adjectives,
pages 276–277 **10**

Comparing with *Good* and *Bad*

┌─ **REMEMBER** THE **RULES** ═══════════════════════

• The words **better** and **worse** are used to compare two things.

*The animal exhibits were **better** than last year.*

*The performers were **worse** than the year before.*

• The words **best** and **worst** are used to compare more than two things.

*The roller coaster is the **best** ride of all.*

*The Ferris wheel is the **worst** ride of all.*

A. Underline the form of *good* or *bad* that is used to compare.

1. Our county fair is the best fair in the state.

2. This year's fair is even better than the one last year.

3. The crowds are worse in the evening than in the afternoon.

4. The worst crowds of all are on the weekends.

5. The rides are the best part of the fair.

B. Rewrite each sentence. Choose the correct form of the adjective in parentheses ( ).

6. My sister thinks the food choices were (good) this year than last.

_____

7. The variety of food was the (good) it has ever been.

_____

8. The hot dogs were (bad) than the hamburgers.

_____

9. My friend thinks cotton candy is the (good) food of all.

_____

10. I think cotton candy is the (bad) food I can eat.

_____

McGraw-Hill Language Arts
Grade 4, Unit 4, Adjectives,
pages 278–279
10

At Home: Ask family members what they like to do best
and what they do not like to do. Write their responses
using forms of *good* and *bad*.

60

Combining Sentences: Adjectives

┌─ **REMEMBER** THE **RULES** ═══════════════════════════

- **Combine sentences** that tell about the same person, place, or thing.
- An **adjective** can be added to one of the sentences.

Chin has a cat.
The cat is gray. ⟩→ *Chin has a **gray** cat.*

└──

A. Write each pair of sentences as one sentence.

1. Mark has a dog. The dog is friendly.

_____

2. His dog can do tricks. The tricks are clever.

_____

3. Cora has a parrot. The parrot is colorful.

_____

4. The parrot lives in a cage. The cage is large.

_____

5. Kim bought an aquarium. The aquarium was empty.

_____

B. Write an adjective to complete each sentence.

6. Jessie has a _____ guinea pig.

7. Jessie built a _____ cage for her guinea pig.

8. Mark bought a _____ iguana.

9. The iguana has a very _____ tail.

10. The iguana has _____ claws.

At Home: Write three pairs of sentences describing a pet you have had or would like to have. Then see if you can **61** combine each pair of sentences.

McGraw-Hill Language Arts
Grade 4, Unit 4, Adjectives,
pages 280–281 /10

Mechanics and Usage: Letter Punctuation

> **REMEMBER** THE **RULES**
>
> - Begin the **greeting** and **closing** of a letter with a **capital letter.**
> - Use a **comma** after the greeting of a friendly letter and the closing.
>   *Dear Midge,*   *Sincerely,*
> - Use a **comma** between the names of a city and state.
>   *Columbus, Ohio*
> - Use a **comma** between the day and year in a date.
>   *January 5, 2002*

A. Write these letter parts. Add the correct punctuation mark or capital letter.

1. dear Jim   _____

2. Sincerely   _____

3. yours truly   _____

4. Boston Massachusetts   _____

5. July 15 2001   _____

6. Dear Mr Johnson   _____

7. detroit michigan   _____

8. september 21 2001   _____

9. your pal   _____

10. dear friend   _____

B. Write the following parts of a letter. Punctuate and capitalize correctly.

11. Write your favorite greeting. _____

12. Write today's date as you would in a letter. _____

13. Write your favorite closing. _____

14. Write your city and state as you would in a letter. _____

15. Write another closing you might use. _____

15 **McGraw-Hill Language Arts**
Grade 4, Unit 4, Adjectives,
pages 282–283

At Home: Look at a letter you have received. It could be a
letter from an advertiser or a friend. Check how the parts of
the letter are punctuated and capitalized.

62

Mixed Review

A. Underline the correct form of the word or words in parentheses ( ).

1. The first half of the talent show was (better, best) than the second half.

2. The dog act was the (worse, worst) of the entire show.

3. The costumes were (fancier, fanciest) than they were last year.

4. The singers were the (more popular, most popular) act of all.

5. The juggling act was the (more unusual, most unusual) I have seen.

B. Write each pair of sentences as one sentence.

6. We had tickets to the talent show. The tickets were free.

_____

7. We saw several acts. The acts were excellent.

_____

8. The singers sang several songs. The songs were popular.

_____

9. The magician performed many acts. The magician's acts were astounding.

_____

10. The audience applauded loudly. The audience was large.

_____

At Home: Think of a place you and your family have been. Write a paragraph about what you saw. Include some comparative adjectives.

63

McGraw-Hill Language Arts
Grade 4, Unit 4, Mixed Review,
pages 284–285   /10

McGraw-Hill School Division

Common Errors: Adjectives

> **REMEMBER** THE **RULES**
>
> - For most short adjectives, add **-er** to compare two people, places, or things. Add **-est** to compare more than two.
>
>   *Cheetahs are **faster** animals than lions.*
>
>   *Cheetahs are the **fastest** land animals of all.*
>
> - For long adjectives, use **more** to compare two people, places, or things. Use **most** to compare more than two.
>
>   *Monkeys are **more popular** than snakes.*
>
>   *Monkeys are the **most playful** of animals.*
>
> - Never use **-er** or **-est** with **more** or **most**.
>
>   *A hippopotamus has a ~~more~~ **bigger** mouth than an alligator*
>
>   *Elephants have the ~~most~~ **longest** tusks of any animal.*

A. Write the correct form of the adjective in parentheses ( ) to complete each sentence.

1. The cheetah is the _____ runner on earth. (fast)

2. The hummingbird is the _____ of all birds. (small)

3. The giraffe is the _____ of all the animals. (tall)

4. Parrots are some of the _____ of all birds. (colorful)

5. An elephant lives a _____ life than a hippopotamus. (long)

B. Complete each sentence by supplying the correct form of an adjective.

6. The ostrich is the _____ of all birds.

7. The leopard is one of the most _____ of all animals.

8. A giraffe is _____ than an elephant.

9. A parrot is more _____ than a sparrow.

10. A mouse is _____ than a squirrel.

/10 **McGraw-Hill Language Arts**
Grade 4, Unit 4, Adjectives
pages 286–287

At Home: Write five sentence that compare different kinds of animals. Be sure you use the correct form of the adjectives that compare.

64

Study Skills: Maps

- A **map** depicts the earth or part of the earth in a special way.
- A **political map** shows borders, a **physical map** shows land features, and a **road map** shows roads.
- On a map, the **compass rose** shows directions, the **scale** shows distances between locations, and the **legend,** or **key,** shows the map symbols.

Use the map to answer the questions. Circle your answer.

1. Which state is just to the west of Vermont?

   New York   New Hampshire

2. What is the capital of Delaware?

   Dover   Philadelphia

3. About how many miles is it from Bangor to Portland, Maine?

   100   200

4. Which body of water lies east of the states of the Northeast?

   Lake Erie   Atlantic Ocean

5. In which direction do you travel from the Adirondack Mountains to the Catskill Mountains?

   north   south

At Home: Think of three questions that the information on the map of the northeastern United States could answer. Try out your questions on a friend or family member.

McGraw-Hill Language Arts
Grade 4, Unit 4, Study Skills,
pages 294–295   5

Vocabulary: Synonyms and Antonyms

> • **Synonyms** are words that have the same or almost the same meaning.
>   *repair/fix*   *cry/sob*   *work/labor*   *press/iron*
> • **Antonyms** are words that have opposite meanings.
>   *stop/go*   *break/mend*   *shout/whisper*   *forget/remember*

A. Choose a synonym from the word box for each underlined word or words. Write the synonym on the line.

disappointed	jumpy	improve	pounds	wild
call	friendly	rarely	tiny	largest

1. I was <u>sad</u> when I didn't make the cheerleading squad. _____

2. My gym teacher said I had to <u>work on</u> my twirling skills. _____

3. I get <u>nervous</u> during tryouts. _____

4. My heart <u>beats</u> fast, and my hands get clammy. _____

5. I think I'll <u>phone</u> Granny to tell her about it. _____

B. Write an antonym for each underlined word. Choose from the word box above.

6. Sharks are <u>domestic</u> animals.

   _____

7. The whale shark is the <u>smallest</u> fish

   of all. _____

8. It is a <u>mean</u> animal. _____

9. It <u>often</u> appears at the water's surface. _____

10. He eats <u>huge</u> plankton and small fish. _____

McGraw-Hill Language Arts
Grade 4, Unit 4, Vocabulary,
pages 296–297

10

At Home: Make a set of cards that show synonyms and antonyms, one word on each card. Mix them up, then have a family member try to match them back together.

Composition: Organization

- It is important to use logical order in your writing so that readers can follow your ideas and understand how they are organized.

- **Time-order words** tell when things happen and in what order. Some time-order words and phrases are: *first, next, then, later, after that, as soon as,* and *a long time ago.*

- **Spatial words** tell where something is found or located. Some spatial words and phrases are: *inside, outside, over, beside, above, near, next to,* and *on top of.*

A. Circle the word or phrase that shows how each sentence is organized. Then place a ✔ in the box labeled **SO** if the sentence is organized by spatial order or **TO** for time order.

	SO	TO
1. Austin loves to make blueberry muffins first thing every morning.	☐	☐
2. He uses the flour stored on top of the refrigerator.	☐	☐
3. Then he goes into the garden and picks fresh blueberries.	☐	☐
4. He mixes the ingredients inside of a big bowl.	☐	☐
5. Soon the muffins will be ready to eat.	☐	☐

B. Complete each sentence with one of the spatial or time-order words in the box. Use each word only once.

as soon as	outside	under	after	then

6. Every morning, Jake goes _____ with his dog Sport.

7. _____ a while, Sport always wants to play with a ball.

8. Jake throws the ball, _____ Sport tries to catch it.

9. Sometimes the ball rolls _____ a bush.

10. _____ Sport catches the ball, his tail wags like crazy.

At Home: Write five sentences that tell about something you like to do when you go outside. Include spatial or time-order words in each sentence.

67

McGraw-Hill Language Arts
Grade 4, Unit 4, Composition Skills,
pages 298–299

/10

McGraw-Hill School Division

Features of Explanatory Writing

A good explanation
- **informs or explains** how to complete a certain task.
- gives **step-by-step directions** in a logical order.
- provides **clear details** that are easy to follow.
- uses **time-order words** or **spatial words** to make the directions clearer.

A. Read the paragraph. Underline the sentence that tells what is being explained.

1. Where are the elephants? Here are directions to the elephant area of the zoo. First, enter the zoo at the pool of sea lions. Stop, if you like, and watch these wonderful creatures swim and dive. Behind the sea lion pool, turn to the right. Then, when you reach the snake and turtle displays, turn to your left. In front of you will be a very large, grassy area. At last, you've found the elephants!

B. Use information from the paragraph to list the animals you would see in order on the way to the elephants.

2. _____

3. _____

4. _____

5. List some of the time-order and spatial words that make this paragraph clearer?

_____

Prewrite: Explanatory Writing

When you use **explanatory writing,** you inform your reader about how to do something. You might explain in writing how to follow a recipe or how to get from school to your home. This kind of writing usually requires directions, step by step. To help organize your ideas, use a **flow chart.**

Plan your own explanatory writing. Brainstorm something you would like to explain, such as how to play a game, bake cookies, or get to the baseball park from your house. Use the flow chart to help organize your thoughts, step by step.

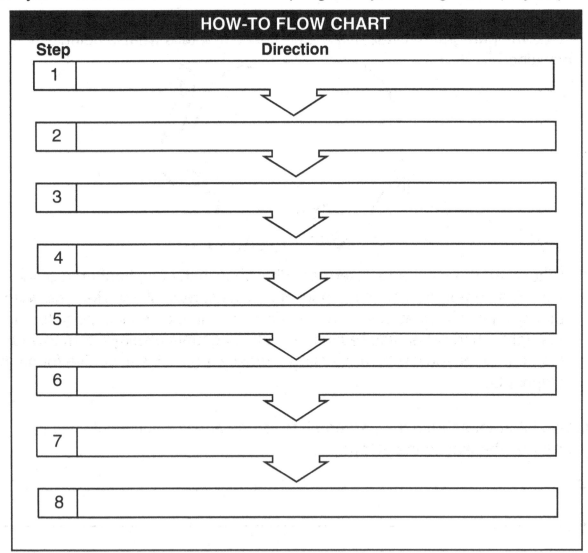

HOW-TO FLOW CHART
Step   **Direction**

CHECKLIST

- Are your step-by-step directions easy to follow?
- Did you leave out any important steps?
- Do you need to do any more research?

At Home: Make up a flow chart to show how you set the dinner table at home. What do you do first, second, and third?

67b

McGraw-Hill Language Arts
Grade 4, Unit 4, Explanatory Writing,
pages 308–309

McGraw-Hill School Division

Revise: Explanatory Writing

A good way to improve, or **revise**, explanatory writing is to add some details or take out text that may confuse your reader. When giving directions to a location, it helps to use spatial words and phrases to help make the directions clearer.

right   left   next to   far from   around   across from   north   west

A. Pretend a new neighbor knocked at your door at 236 Maple Street. The neighbor asked for directions to get to the nearest mall. You wrote the following directions for your neighbor. Study the map. Then add details to your directions to improve them.

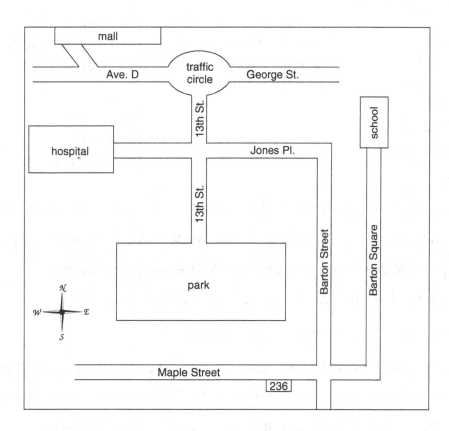

Go down to Barton. Turn and go to Jones Place. Turn on 13th and

head toward the traffic circle. Whatever you do, don't go onto George St.

It will lead you out of town. Keep going around the circle. That will lead

you directly to the mall.

B. Use the changes you marked to rewrite the directions on another piece of paper.

McGraw-Hill Language Arts
Grade 4, Unit 4, Explanatory Writing,
pages 314-315

At Home: Write directions explaining how to get from your house to the nearest mall, library, or supermarket. Then revise your writing.

67c

Proofread: Explanatory Writing

PROOFREADING MARKS
⌗ new paragraph
∧ add
৭ take out
☰ Make a capital letter.
/ Make a small letter.
ⓢⓟ Check the spelling.
⊙ Add a period.

After you have revised your explanatory writing, you will need to **proofread** it to correct any errors. Reread for punctuation. Check carefully for spelling mistakes. Look for capitals at the beginning of each sentence, and look at the beginnings of street names, city names, and dates.

A. Pretend you wrote the following letter to a friend. Now it is time to proofread it. Use the proofreading marks from the box to mark any errors you find.

587 langston Rd.
Short Hills, nJ
Oct. 12 2003

Dear Mike,

I was so hapy to get your letter. I loved the jokes you sent. Now I have something to share with you I learned a new game toady. here is what you do:

1) The first player leaves the room while the others choose a homophone, such as the word *tide (tied)*. That is the secret word or words.

2) Then the first player returns to the group.

3) The rest of the players give clues by saying sentences using the secret word but they don't say the word *tide*. They use a different word. Here is an example: "In the ninth inning, the score was (clock)."

4) The first player has three turns to guesses the secret homophone. Then the next player goes.

Well, I have to go do my homework now. Write soon.

your friend,
Charles

B. On another sheet of paper, rewrite the letter with your corrections.

At Home: Write a letter to a friend. Include a joke or riddle or explain how to play a game. Then proofread your work.

67d

McGraw-Hill Language Arts
Grade 4, Unit 4, Explanatory Writing,
pages 318–319

10

Pronouns

REMEMBER THE RULES

- A pronoun is a word that replaces one or more nouns. It should always match the noun it refers to.

    A **geologist** spoke **to the students.**
    He spoke to **them.**

A. Write the pronoun that refers to the underlined noun. Write **S** if the pronoun is singular, or **P** if the pronoun is plural.

1. As the <u>students</u> listened to the teacher, they learned many things.

   _____

2. The <u>man</u> knew a lot about rocks, and he showed us several samples.

   _____

3. The igneous <u>rock</u> was dense, and it had a dark black color.

   _____

4. Most of the sedimentary <u>rocks</u> had layered stripes going through them.

   _____

5. My <u>friends</u> were glad the teacher had enough rock samples for each of us.

   _____

B. Write a pronoun that can take the place of the underlined word or words.

6. I didn't know a <u>geologist</u> could be as interesting as _____ was.

7. The <u>children</u> know that's where _____ will find igneous rocks.

8. She will ask her <u>father</u> if _____ can take students there.

9. If the girl's <u>father</u> is able to go, the students will thank _____.

10. Before <u>you and I</u> can find a special type of rock, _____ have to learn where to look for it.

marble

azurite

malachite
flourite

McGraw-Hill Language Arts
Grade 4, Unit 5, Pronouns,
pages 344–345

10

At Home: Tell a family member whether each pronoun you wrote in Part B is singular or plural.

Name_____ Date_____ **Practice** (69)

Subject Pronouns

```
┌─ REMEMBER THE RULES ══════════════════════════════════╗
│ • A subject pronoun is used as the subject of a sentence. It shows
│   whom or what a sentence is about.
│ • A subject pronoun can be singular or plural.
│     Singular: I, you, he, she, it
│         She plans to attend the sports banquet with her parents.
│     Plural: we, you, they
│         They will sit with six other people at a large table.
└────────────────────────────────────────────────────────┘
```

A. Underline the subject pronoun in each sentence.

1. I am planning an awards banquet for the coaches.

2. They told us our families should attend.

3. We asked Coach Jeffers to present our awards.

4. He enjoys recognizing his favorite athletes.

5. You should ask Susan to bring her camera.

6. It will be nice to have some pictures taken.

7. Will she be happy to do this favor for us?

B. Write the subject pronoun that will complete the second sentence.

8. Will Donald win an award? _____ won last year.

9. The coach brought his wife. _____ will help him.

10. Everyone will take home a trophy. _____ will like that.

11. I saw the best effort award. _____ is the biggest trophy!

12. Lisa deserves to win the award. _____ works hard!

13. Alex, call our house if you need a ride. _____ can ask us to pick you up.

14. My mother won't mind. _____ live very close to you.

15. Please sit with me. _____ will save a seat for you.

At Home: For each subject pronoun you wrote in Part B, underline the noun in the first sentence that the pronoun refers to.

69

McGraw-Hill Language Arts
Grade 4, Unit 5, Pronouns,
pages 346–347

15

McGraw-Hill School Division

Object Pronouns

┌─ **REMEMBER** THE **RULES** ─────────────────────────────┐

- An **object pronoun** is a pronoun used after an action verb or after a word such as *for, at, of, with,* or *to.*
- Object pronouns can be singular or plural.

   Singular: me, you, him, her, it

   Plural: us, you, them

   *High school counselors will <u>help</u> **him** plan his college search.*

   *Most students choose colleges that are perfect <u>for</u> **them.***

└──┘

A. Write an object pronoun for each sentence.

1. College recruiters may contact _____ someday.

2. You will want to visit with _____ when they do.

3. I hope that they will grant you and _____ an interview.

4. They will expect both of _____ to take a test.

5. We will work hard to prepare for _____.

6. One boy said he brought his calculator with _____.

B. Write the letter **C** next to the sentence that uses the correct object pronoun.

7. _____ Angie told us she applied to several colleges.

   _____ Angie told we she applied to several colleges.

8. _____ A scholarship was offered to her.

   _____ A scholarship was offered to she.

9. _____ Angie must sign and return the offer to they.

   _____ Angie must sign and return the offer to them.

10. _____ Our counselor has some suggestions for you and I.

   _____ Our counselor has some suggestions for you and me.

McGraw-Hill Language Arts
10 **Grade 4, Unit 5, Pronouns,**
pages 348–349

At Home: Underline the word that comes before each correct object pronoun in Part B. Tell whether the underlined word is a verb or a special word.

70

Mechanics and Usage: Punctuation in Dialogue

REMEMBER THE **RULES**

- **Dialogue** is the exact words spoken by the characters in a story.
- **Quotation marks** are placed at the beginning and end of the words being spoken.
- A speaker's words begin with a **capital letter.**
- A **new paragraph** begins when a new person speaks.

    "I think it is about time to plan our dream home," said Dad.

    "I'll ask Aunt Kay whom she used last year," said Mom.

Rewrite and correct each sentence that needs quotation marks and capital letters. If a sentence is correct, write *Correct* on the line.

1. There are so many decisions to make, Dad said.

   _____

2. Let's look in magazines for ideas, Mom suggested.

   _____

3. The architect asked, how do you like the plans I drew up?

   _____

4. the family room is going to be beautiful! said my mom.

   _____

5. it certainly looks big enough, she added.

   _____

6. My father nodded his head in approval.

   _____

7. The architect asks, do you like where I placed the garage?

   _____

8. My dad responds, yes, but where is the driveway going to be?

   _____

9. The architect told them that he put it on the left side of the house.

   _____

10. That will work out well for us, Dad answered.

    _____

At Home: Look in the newspaper for examples of dialogue. Underline the exact words people are saying.

71

McGraw-Hill Language Arts
Grade 4, Unit 5, Pronouns,
pages 350–351

/10

Mixed Review

┌─ **REMEMBER** THE **RULES** ═══════════════════════════════

- A **subject pronoun** is used as the subject of a sentence. *We often visit the park near our house.*

- An **object pronoun** follows an action verb or words such as *for, at, of, with,* and *to. Sometimes my grandparents go with* **us.**

- Use **quotation marks** at the beginning and end of a person's exact words. *"Who wants to see the concert in the park?" Mom asked.*

A. Complete the sentence pairs with a subject or object pronoun.

1. My friend and I like to go to the park. _____ like to watch what's going on.

2. There are many squirrels in the park. _____ chase each other through the trees.

3. Once we saw a raccoon. _____ slowly lumbered across our path.

4. Some people go to the park to look at birds. There are many different kinds of _____ to see.

5. Once my mom saw a rare kind of swallow. _____ said it was very beautiful.

B. Add quotation marks and capital letters to rewrite each sentence.

6. let's go to the boat pond, mark said.

_____

7. they are having a model boat race today, luis explained.

_____

8. look! mark yelled. there are about a dozen boats in the water.

_____

9. haven't you ever been here before? asked luis.

_____

10. not since yesterday, laughed mark.

_____

☑10 **McGraw-Hill Language Arts**
Grade 4, Unit 5, Mixed Review,
pages 352–353

At Home: Write down a conversation between you and a family member. Add quotation marks around exact words. Use some subject and object pronouns.

72

Pronoun-Verb Agreement

REMEMBER THE **RULES**

- To make most action verbs in the present tense agree with the pronouns *he, she,* or *it,* add *-s* or *-es.*

    She plan<u>s</u> *to cook steaks for her guests.*

    He push<u>es</u> *the baby carriage in the park.*

- When using the pronouns *I, we, you,* and ***they,*** do not add *-s* or *-es* to present-tense action verbs.

    They *plan to arrive at seven o'clock.*

    We *push the baby carriages in the park.*

A. Write the correct present-tense verb from the pair in parentheses.

1. Sometimes we (ask, asks) our friends Ellen and Marty to help. _____

2 It (make, makes) entertaining easier when you have help. _____

3 Marty (wishes, wish) to prepare the rice. _____

4. Ellen knows how to bake. She (want, wants) to bring dessert. _____

5. I (figure, figures) we have enough food for eight guests. _____

B. Rewrite the second sentence of each pair of sentences using the correct present-tense form of the verb in parentheses.

6. Marty brought his rice steamer. It _____ on the countertop. (fit)

_____

7. Ellen's pies look delicious. I would like to _____ a slice right now! (cut)

_____

8. Our guests are prompt. They _____ on time. (arrive)

_____

9. A buzzer from the kitchen interrupts us. It _____ loudly. (ring)

_____

10. Ellen runs to the kitchen. She _____ the roast hasn't burned. (hope)

_____

At Home: Replace nouns with pronouns in the first sentences of Part B. Say each new sentence aloud to a family member.

73

McGraw-Hill Language Arts
Grade 4, Unit 5, Pronouns,
pages 354–355

10

McGraw-Hill School Division

Combining Sentences

┌─ **REMEMBER** THE **RULES** ────────────────────────────────

- You can combine sentences by joining two subject or object **pronouns.**

  You plan for a trip. **I** plan for a trip. → **You and I** plan for a trip.

  Climate affects **you.** → Climate affects **you and me.**
  Climate affects **me.**

└──

A. Join the pronouns in each pair of sentences. Write them on the lines.

1. He can describe what climate is. I can describe what climate is. _____

2. Will rain bother him? Will rain bother her? _____

3. I will wear new clothing. You will wear new clothing. _____

4 We prefer cotton. They prefer cotton. _____

5. You will select light-colored clothes. I will select light-colored clothes.

   _____

B. Rewrite each pair of sentences as one new sentence.

6. You planted cactus. He planted cactus.

   _____

7. They harvested corn. We harvested corn.

   _____

8. She enjoys the warm climate. He enjoys the warm climate.

   _____

9. Garments protect them from the cold. Garments protect us from the cold.

   _____

10. Climate influences the kind of home you live in. Climate influences the kind
    of home I live in.

    _____

McGraw-Hill Language Arts
Grade 4, Unit 5, Pronouns,
pages 356–357

At Home: Rewrite each pair of sentences in Part A as one.

74

Possessive Pronouns

┌─ **REMEMBER** THE **RULES** ─────────────────────

• **Possessive pronouns** replace possessive nouns.

• Some **possessive pronouns** are used before nouns. Others stand alone.

    *Dale is scheduling **his** dentist appointment.*

    *Annie is scheduling **hers**.*

└───

A. Underline the possessive pronoun in each sentence.

1. It was time for his annual checkup at the dentist's office.

2. Annie thought it was her time to go, also.

3. Dale and Annie called their dentist for an appointment.

4. When could he fit them in for their checkups?

5. No one's schedule is busier than his.

6. The receptionist asked them, "When is your schedule free?"

7. She told them that Monday was her only day off from work.

8. Dale said that was his best day to come in also.

9. The woman said, "It looks like his first opening is next Monday."

10. I looked at my calendar to see if we were busy.

B. Complete each sentence with a possessive pronoun.

11. We decided to rearrange _____ plans.

12. The receptionist put our names in _____ book.

13. The receptionist told Dale _____ teeth would be cleaned first.

14. Then she told me _____ would be worked on next.

15. _____ would be the first appointments that day, she told us.

Mechanics and Usage: Contractions: Pronouns and Verbs

┌─ **REMEMBER** THE **RULES** ─────────────────────

- A **contraction** can be formed from a pronoun and a verb.
- Do not confuse *it's, you're, they're* with *its, your,* and *their.*

   It's *time for the squirrel to prepare for winter.*
   Its *coat is brown and gray.*

   You're *coming to the park.*   ***They're*** *coming along, too.*
   Your *jacket is unbuttoned.*   ***Their*** *jackets all have hoods.*

A. Write the word in parentheses that means the same as the given words.

1. I am (I'm, Im's) _____   **9.** I would (I've, I'd) _____

2. belonging to you   **10.** belonging to them

   (your, you're) _____   (there's, their) _____

3. he is (his, he's) _____   **11.** they are (there, they're) _____

4. I had (I'm, I'd) _____   **12.** you are (your, you're) _____

5. I have (I've, I'd) _____   **13.** she is (she's, she'd) _____

6. belonging to it (it's, its) _____   **14.** she will (she's, she'll) _____

7. he will (he'll, he'd) _____   **15.** she would (she'd, she'll) _____

8. it is (its, it's) _____   **16.** I will (I'd, I'll) _____

B. Rewrite each sentence using a contraction.

17. <u>It is</u> time for some animals to hibernate.

_____

18. <u>They are</u> looking for a place to sleep during the winter.

_____

19. <u>You will</u> also see them gathering nuts and seeds.

_____

20. <u>It will</u> keep them busy until winter snows cover the ground.

_____

McGraw-Hill Language Arts
Grade 4, Unit 5, Pronouns,
pages 360–361
20

At Home: Write sentences using five contractions from
Part A.

76

Mixed Review

A. Circle the correct form of the verb in parentheses ( ).

1. Entertainment (come, comes) in many different forms.

2. It (improve, improves) the quality of life for most people.

3. Television (entertain, entertains) some people for hours.

4. Others (read, reads) books for enjoyment and relaxation.

5. They (take, takes) their entertainment wherever they go.

B. Rewrite each sentence. Form contractions from the underlined words and substitute possessive pronouns for underlined possessive nouns.

6. You have never watched Terri's and my television program?

_____

7. I have got to read my sister's latest poems.

_____

8. We are going to see Joe and Andrew's movie thriller.

_____

9. It is going to be an interesting night at Tony's art show.

_____

10. They are going to get tickets for Michael's and Betty's play.

_____

At Home: Think about what kind of entertainment your family and friends enjoy. Write a sentence about each person. Include some possessive pronouns and contractions.

McGraw-Hill Language Arts
Grade 4, Unit 5, Mixed Review,
pages 362–363

10

McGraw-Hill School Division

Common Errors: Pronouns

┌─ **REMEMBER** THE **RULES** ═══════════════════════════════

- Use a **subject pronoun** (*I, you, he, she, it, we, they*) as the subject of a sentence.

  We *want to take a trip to see the pyramids.*

- Use an **object pronoun** (*me, you, him, her, it, us, them*) after an action verb or after words such as *for, at, of, with,* or *to*.

  My family has always wanted to see **them.**

- An apostrophe shows where a letter has been left out of a contraction of a pronoun and a verb. Possessive pronouns do not have apostrophes.

  Such a trip would be learning at **its** *best.*

A. Circle the correct pronoun in parentheses ( ) to complete each sentence.

1. The Egyptian pyramids amaze (I, me).

2. (They, Them) were built as tombs for Egyptian kings.

3. Some of (they, them) were built about 4,500 years ago.

4. A king was buried in a pyramid to protect (he, him) after he died.

5. The pyramid of Cheops is the largest of (they, them).

6. (He, Him) was an Egyptian pharaoh.

7. The pyramid is 450 feet tall, and (its, it's) base covers about 13 acres.

8. (We, Us) can visit the great pyramids in Giza in Egypt.

9. (I, me) am planning a trip to see them next year.

10. Why don't (we, us) travel there together?

B. Write a pronoun to complete each sentence correctly.

11. The agency planned a tour just for _____.

12. _____ are going to see the pyramids in the fall.

13. The agency is sending along _____ best tour guide.

14. _____ will tell _____ about the pyramids.

15. My friends and _____ can hardly wait.

McGraw-Hill Language Arts
Grade 4, Unit 5, Pronouns
pages 364–365

At Home: Write five sentences about a place you have been to with your family or a friend. Include a pronoun in each sentence.

78

Study Skills: Dictionary

A dictionary includes

- **guide words** that show the first and last entries on a page.

- **entry words** that appear alphabetically.

- a **respelling** for pronunciation,
  an abbreviation for the **part of speech,**
  a **definition,** and often an **example sentence** for every entry word.

- a **pronunciation key** that explains respellings of words in entries,
  usually found at the bottom of every other dictionary page.

Answer these questions about using a dictionary. Circle or write your answers on the lines. Refer to a dictionary if you need to.

1. Between which two guide words would the word *pioneer* appear?

   pinafore/pinion   pinstripe/pipe   pique/pitch

2. Between which two guide words would *impression* appear?

   imperial/impinge   impish/impresario   impress/improvise

3. What do the letters *v.* or *n.* in a dictionary entry tell you?

   pronunciation   part of speech   guide words

4. What symbol is used to show the pronunciation of the word *bake*?

   _____

5. In which order would you find the following words listed?

   gild   ghoul   giant   geyser   ghost

   _____

   _____

At Home: Study a dictionary entry for a word that is unfamiliar to you. Then, try to use that word in your next conversation or your next piece of writing.

McGraw-Hill Language Arts
Grade 4, Unit 5, Study Skills,
pages 372–373   5

McGraw-Hill School Division

Vocabulary: Homophones and Homographs

- Homophones are words that sound alike but have different spellings and different meanings.

    kernel   colonel   tale tail   weigh   way   brake break

- Homographs are words that are spelled the same but have different meanings and often have different pronunciations.

    When the baby <u>tears</u> my homework, you can see my <u>tears</u>.

    My mother asks me to <u>close</u> the door that is <u>close</u> to the window.

A. Choose a word from the word box that fits each definition.

ate	chest	close	clothes	eight	read	scene
seen	weak	week	wind	wood	would	

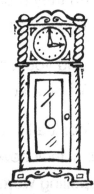

1. it comes from a tree: _____

2. past tense of will: _____

3. moving air: _____

4. without energy: _____

5. part of a play: _____

B. Complete each sentence with the correct word from the word box.

6. It is time to _____ the grandfather clock.

7. At _____ o'clock, I get to watch my favorite TV show.

8. Afterwards Dad will _____ a chapter of *Treasure Island* to me and my brother.

9. Then I will take the _____ that I will wear tomorrow out of my closet.

10. I will set everything on my cedar _____.

McGraw-Hill Language Arts
10 Grade 4, Unit 5, Vocabulary,
pages 374–375

At Home: Look in the dictionary for two ways to pronounce
perfect. Then write a sentence with each homograph.

80

Composition: Writing Dialogue

- **Dialogue** is conversation between two or more characters in a story.
- Put **quotation marks** around a character's exact words.
- Always tell who is speaking by using words such as *said Maria* or *he explained.*
- Each time there is a new speaker, begin a new paragraph.
- Capitalize the first word in a quotation.
- Put the end punctuation inside the quotation.

   "It's the most beautiful bracelet I've ever seen," cried Luisa.

- If the speaker's name comes first, put a comma before the quotation.

A. Read the paragraphs. Put a quotation mark before the first word of every quotation.

1-5. As they prepared for school, Monica said, Tamika, I can't find my list of spelling words for this week."

   Did you look under the bed?" her sister Tamika asked. A few moments later Tamika added, You might be surprised if you do look."

   Monica lifted the hem of the bright orange quilt. She exclaimed, Oh, no!" Mittens, their new kitten, was shredding paper to bits. Monica said, I memorized the spelling words for the week, but can you help me check the spelling in the dictionary, Tamika?"

B. The dialogue in the sentences that follow need punctuation and capitalization. Add quotation marks, capital letters, and punctuation.

6. Tamika picked up a dictionary and said, Monica tell me the first word on your list

7. The first word is *monopoly,* Monica replied.

8. What does that word mean   Tamika asked her sister.

9. My favorite board game   Monica exclaimed.

10. Tamika said, monica the dictionary has another meaning for *monopoly*

At Home: Continue the conversation between Monica and Tamika. Use the rules for dialogue from the box on this page.

McGraw-Hill Language Arts
Grade 4, Unit 5, Composition Skills,
pages 376–377

81   /10

McGraw-Hill School Division

Features of a Story

A good story
- has **characters** that move the action along.
- has a **beginning, middle,** and **end.**
- has a plot **with a problem** that is solved at the end.
- describes a **setting,** telling where and when the story takes place.
- uses **dialogue words** that show how the characters are speaking.

A. 1.- 2. Read the story. Underline the name of the main character and the problem he or she faces.

    "Oh, no!" Nelson cried out. Unfortunately, nothing he said could bring back his kite. It flew up and out of the park.

    "Excuse me," a friendly little girl stepped up to Nelson. He was standing on the park path with his eyes fixed to the sky. "What are you looking for?"

    "I lost my kite," Nelson said. "Not just any old kite, but a birthday present from my Uncle Shandon."

    The little girl told Nelson not to worry.

    He thanked the kind little girl and then decided to go home for lunch.

    When Nelson opened the door to his house, he called, "I'm home!" Strangely, his mother didn't answer. Nelson walked to the kitchen and looked out the back door. There was his mother on a ladder, climbing down from the roof.

    "Look what our old chimney stopped in mid flight!" Nelson's mother said.

B. Use the information from the story to answer the following questions.

3. What is the setting of the story at the beginning? _____

4. What event forms the middle of the story?

_____

5. What event helps solve the problem at the end of the story?

_____

_____

⬚ **McGraw-Hill Language Arts**
5 **Grade 4, Unit 5, Story,**
pages 384–385

At Home: Write a story about a problem that could happen to you one day in the park. Try to include dialogue in the beginning, middle, or end of your story.

81a

Prewrite: Story

A **story** is a form of writing that is created from the author's imagination. The purpose is to entertain readers. A story should have a beginning, middle, and a satisfying ending. A **story map** will help you list the events of your story.

Plan your own story by brainstorming ideas for a plot, setting, and characters. Think about a problem the character or characters might have to solve. Figure out a way for them to solve the problem. Then fill in the story map.

STORY MAP

Title:
Setting:
Characters:
Problem:

Events

Solution:

CHECKLIST

- Have you listed story ideas from your imagination?
- Have you selected an interesting setting and characters?
- Are your ideas organized?

At Home: Think about one of your favorite storybook characters. Write a paragraph stating why this character is so interesting to you.

McGraw-Hill Language Arts
Grade 4, Unit 5, Story,
pages 386–387

Revise: Story

One way to **revise** your story writing is to elaborate. You can elaborate by adding details to your story. You might describe the setting and the characters with more details. Another way to elaborate a story is by adding dialogue.

Dialogue words: cried, retorted, asked, chuckled, whispered.

Draft: Martha told everyone she wanted to go to the museum, but she also wanted to visit the Statue of Liberty. Bill told her she had to choose.

Revise: Martha stood up and announced to everyone in class, "I want to go to the science museum, but I also want to visit the Statue of Liberty."

Bill told her, "Martha, you have to choose."

Revise the following beginning paragraphs from this familiar story by adding details and dialogue. Use another sheet of paper if you need it.

There was once a young girl who wore a cape with a hood. She was on her way to her grandmother's house. Along the way she met a wolf who asked where she was going. The girl told the wolf.

The wolf ran to the grandmother's house. He put the grandmother in the closet. Then he waited for the girl to come.

_____

_____

_____

_____

_____

_____

_____

_____

_____

_____

_____

At Home: Write an original story without dialogue. Then revise the story and include dialogue.

Proofread: Story

⌗	new paragraph
∧	add
ઉ	take out
═	Make a capital letter.
/	Make a small letter.
ⓢⓟ	Check the spelling.
⊙	Add a period.

After you revise your story, you will need to **proofread** it to find and correct any errors. When you proofread your story you should:
• Correct spelling errors.
• Correct run-on and incomplete sentences.
• Use quotation marks around a speaker's exact words.
• Punctuate the dialogue properly.

A. Read this story. Use the proofreading marks from the box to mark any errors you find.

Martha and her class were on the ferry heading toward Liberty Island. the home of the Statue of Liberty. She and Bill was sitting on the outside part of the ferry when the wind whipped up. Bill's favorite baseball cap flew off his head. it twirled and spun until it finally landed in the cold waters of New York Harbor.

Martha said, "don't worry, you can always get another cap."

Bill said, "Not really. That cap was a gift from from my grandfather.

Martha said, "Oh, Bill, I am so sorry "

Then right before their eyes, a huge seagull swept down into the water and picked up the cap with its beak. It flew toward the ferry railing and it sat right in front of where Martha and Bill stood.

Bill quickly grabbed the cap. "Thank you" he said. Then he and Martha watched the seagull flew into the horizon.

B. Use the corrections you marked to rewrite the story on another sheet of paper.

At Home: Write another ending to the story and proofread your writing.

81d

McGraw-Hill Language Arts
Grade 4, Unit 5, Story,
pages 396–397

10

McGraw-Hill School Division

Adverbs That Tell *How*

┌─ **REMEMBER** THE **RULES** ──────────────────
│ • An **adverb** tells more about a verb.
│ • Some adverbs tell how an action has been done.
│ • Many adverbs end in *–ly*.
│   *Beth **thoughtfully** chose a topic for her science paper.*
└─────────────────────────────────────

A. Write the adverb that describes the underlined verb.

1. Beth eagerly <u>reads</u> her chemistry books. _____

2. Chemistry usually <u>deals</u> with the makeup of substances. _____

3. Chemistry students diligently <u>study</u> the names of elements. _____

4. Beth carefully <u>researched</u> the topic of gases. _____

5. She completely <u>understands</u> what elements make up water. _____

B. Underline the verb and write the adverb.

6. Sara expertly identified the properties of gas. _____

7. An empty jar really contains matter. _____

8. Ordinarily people call those gases air. _____

9. Young children usually recognize ice as a solid. _____

10. All elements behave differently. _____

11. Liquids always take the shape of their containers. _____

12. Solids consistently maintain their shapes. _____

13. Balloons easily fill with a gas so we know gases take up space. _____

14. Microscopes help scientists view molecules closely. _____

15. Teachers frequently use a model of the atom to help their students.

_____

McGraw-Hill Language Arts
Grade 4, Unit 6, Adverbs,
[15] pages 420–421

At Home: Rewrite each sentence in Part A using a different adverb.

Adverbs That Tell *When* or *Where*

┌─ **REMEMBER** THE **RULES** ─────────────────────────

• An **adverb** tells more about a verb. You know that an adverb can tell how. An adverb can also tell when or where an action takes place.

*Travelers **often** tour the island of Oahu.* (tells when)

*The rainforests **outside** the city are filled with beautiful birds.* (tells where)

└──

Write the adverb and underline the verb it describes. Some verbs are formed with two words.

1. A volcano called Mauna Loa is located here. _____

2. Mauna Loa irregularly erupts with streams of fiery lava. _____

3 The unpredictable volcanic activity discourages people from living

   there. _____

4. Oahu always draws both tourists and immigrants. _____

5. Historically, the name Pearl Harbor has significance. _____

6. Naturally, it reminds us of the United States' entry into World War II.

   _____

7. Oahu proudly claims Honolulu,

   the state capital. _____

8. Pearl Harbor is shown clearly on the

   map. _____

9. Visitors usually enjoy the islands'

   scenic beauty. _____

10. Brilliantly colored flowers readily flourish . _____

At Home: Rewrite any three sentences of your choice using a different adverb.

83

McGraw-Hill Language Arts
Grade 4, Unit 6, Adverbs,
pages 422–423   10

McGraw-Hill School Division

Adverbs That Compare

┌─ **REMEMBER** THE **RULES** ─────────────────────────────────

- **Adverbs** can be used to make comparisons.
- Add *–er* to short adverbs to compare two actions. Add *–est* to compare more than two actions.

    *A lion runs **fast.***

    *A pronghorn antelope runs **faster** than a lion.*

    *The cheetah runs the **fastest** of all land animals.*

└──

A. Write the correct form of the adverb in parentheses to complete the sentence.

1. The elephant stands _____ than the rhinoceros. (tallest, taller).

2. Of all mammals, the blue whale grows the _____. (largest, larger)

3. The hyrax appears _____ than a guinea pig. (smallest, smaller)

4. A lion lives _____ than a leopard. (longer, longest)

5. Some mammals grasp _____ with their hands than with their feet. (tightest, tighter)

B. Write a form of the adverb in parentheses that best completes the sentence.

6. Monkeys and opossums grasp _____ with their tails. (tight)

7. Of all monkeys, the tailless potto grips the _____ with its hands and feet. (strong)

8. The giant anteater has the _____ tongue of all mammals. (long)

9. The Asian elephant is _____ in weight than the African elephant. (light)

10. Bats fly _____ than flying lemurs. (high)

McGraw-Hill Language Arts
10 Grade 4, Unit 6, Adverbs,
pages 424–425

At Home: Decide what mammal is your favorite animal. Write phrases with adverbs that compare it to other animals.

84

More Adverbs That Compare

┌─ **REMEMBER** THE **RULES** ─────────────────────────────
- Longer **adverbs** and adverbs that end in *–ly* can be used with the words *more* and *most* to form comparisons.
- Use *more* to compare two actions. Use *most* to compare more than two actions.

  Jennifer competed **more energetically** *than Ali.*

  Among all the runners, Deanna competed **most energetically.**
└──

A. Underline the verb and circle the complete adverb.

1. Of all students, Sean approaches school most seriously.

2. Sean studies more diligently than his brother.

3. He answers test questions more successfully than others do.

4. Krista is treated more warmly by her friends than her tennis coach.

5. Krista should practice tennis more regularly than she has been.

B. Rewrite each sentence using the correct form of the adverb.

6. Of all members on the cross country team, Sara wins (more, most) regularly.

_____

7. Sara runs (more, most) willingly at practice than her friend does.

_____

8. Her new running shoes fit (more, most) comfortably than her old ones.

_____

9. She reached the finish line (more, most) quickly this time than last week.

_____

10. Her dad cheered for her (more, most) enthusiastically of all.

_____

McGraw-Hill School Division

At Home: For each sentence in Part B, tell a family member who or what the adverb is comparing.

85

**McGraw-Hill Language Arts
Grade 4, Unit 6, Adverbs,
pages 426–427** / 10

Mechanics and Usage: *Good* and *Well*

> ┌─ **REMEMBER** THE **RULES** ─────────────────────────
> - The adjective *good* describes a noun.
>   *A **good** magnet will pick up paper clips.*
> - The adverb *well* tells more about a verb.
>   *Some magnets work **well**.*
> - ***Well*** is used as an adjective when referring to someone's health.
>   *I am **well** today.*

A. Write *C* next to the sentence that uses the word *good* or *well* correctly.

1. _____ Magnets are good for picking up small metal objects.

   _____ Magnets are well for picking up small metal objects.

2. _____ You know good how a magnet works.

   _____ You know well how a magnet works.

3. _____ A well bar magnet has two poles.

   _____ A good bar magnet has two poles.

4. _____ A compass is a good example of a
   small bar magnet.

   _____ A compass is a well example of a
   small bar magnet.

5. _____ The tip of a good compass needle always points north.

   _____ The tip of a well compass needle always points north.

B. Complete each sentence with *good* or *well*.

6. Bar magnets are _____ for keeping doors closed.

7. Horseshoe magnets work _____ in slot car motors.

8. Disk magnets in radio speakers distribute electrical impulses _____.

9. Some people believe wearing magnets will help you feel _____.

10. No scientific evidence proves magnets are _____ for you.

McGraw-Hill Language Arts
Grade 4, Unit 6, Adverbs,
pages 428–429
10

At Home: Explain to a family member why each sentence
in Part A is either correct or incorrect.

86

Mixed Review

┌─ **REMEMBER** THE **RULES** ─────────────────────────────────┐

- An **adverb** adds details about a verb by telling *how, who,* or *where.*
  *I **suddenly** remembered my mother's birthday.*
- Short **adverbs** ending in *-er* and *-est* can be used to make comparisons. *I plan **harder** for this year's party than last year's.*
- Long **adverbs** and adverbs ending in *-y* can be used with *more* and *most* to make comparisons.

└──┘

A. Underline adverbs. Write whether the adverb tells *how, when,* or *where.*

1. My mother's birthday is nearly here. _____

2. We secretly planned a birthday party for her. _____

3. We carefully chose a birthday present that she would like. _____

4. We had the store elaborately wrap her gift. _____

5. We went there because we knew they would do a neat job. _____

6. I cleverly hide the gift where she would never find it. _____

7. Today, my aunt made a beautiful cake for the party. _____

8. The party guests came here for the celebration. _____

9. Everyone quickly signed my mother's birthday card. _____

10. She was really surprised when she walked into the room. _____

B. Choose the correct adverb in parentheses to complete each sentence.

11. I work _____ of all at putting this party together. (harder, hardest)

12. Of all my parties, this one went the _____. (more smoothly, most smoothly.)

13. The quests arrived _____ this year than last year. (more quickly, most quickly)

14. They stayed _____ this time than last time. (longer, longest)

15. The party ended _____ than the one before. (later, latest)

At Home: Think of a party you or a family member have had. Write a paragraph about it. Include some adverbs and circle each one.

87

McGraw-Hill Language Arts
Grade 4, Unit 6, Mixed Review,
pages 430–431 / 15

Negatives

```
┌─ REMEMBER THE RULES ─────────────────────────────┐
│ • A negative is a word that means "no." Many negatives contain the    │
│   word no within them                                                 │
│        not, nobody, nowhere, none, no one                             │
│ • Some negatives include the contraction –n't.                        │
│        can't, don't, won't, isn't                                     │
└───────────────────────────────────────────────────┘
```

A. Write the negative word that appears in each sentence.

1. Try not to have a negative outlook. _____

2. No one is more discouraging than a pessimist. _____

3. Complaining usually accomplishes nothing. _____

4. Looking at things the wrong way will get you nowhere. _____

5. Nobody wants to be with someone who is gloomy. _____

B. Rewrite each sentence using the correct word in parentheses.

6. No one is going to talk negatively around me (no, any) more.

_____

7. I don't want to hear (nothing, anything) that is discouraging.

_____

8. I'm not (ever, never) going to listen to a critical word.

_____

9. Isn't it time we tried (nothing, something) to correct this problem?

_____

10. Wouldn't (nobody, anybody) like to join me?

_____

At Home: Write a list of rules for choosing a positive attitude. Include negatives in your list of rules. For example: *Nobody should whine.*

Prepositions

┌─ **REMEMBER** THE **RULES** ════════════════════════════

- A **preposition** comes before a noun or pronoun. It relates the noun or pronoun to another word in the sentence.

    *You might choose a trip **to** Argentina one day.*

    *Argentina is the second-largest country **in** South America.*

    *Huge ranches are found **around** the Pampas and Patagonia.*

A. Write the preposition in each sentence.

1. Argentina follows Brazil in population and area. _____

2. The Andes Mountains run along the country's western boundary. _____

3. A grassy plain called the Pampas appears near the middle. _____

4. Cowhands, called *gauchos*, herded cattle throughout the Pampas.

    _____

5. Argentina is known for its well-aged beef. _____

B. Choose the correct preposition to complete each sentence.

6. Argentina was once (across, under) Spanish rule. _____

7. Many people emigrated (from, under)

    Europe. _____

8. Many immigrants settled (near, under)

    Buenos Aires. _____

9. Most people speak Spanish (behind,

    throughout) Argentina. _____

10. (In, Near) Brazil, however, the people

    speak Portuguese. _____

At Home: Choose five prepositions from above and write sentences with them.

89

McGraw-Hill Language Arts
Grade 4, Unit 6, Adverbs,
pages 434–435 /10

Prepositional Phrases

REMEMBER THE RULES

- A **prepositional phrase** is a group of words that begins with a preposition and ends with a noun or a pronoun.

*Most people have a physical exam **on** a regular basis.*

A. In each sentence, write the preposition. Then underline the noun or pronoun that follows it.

1. Doctors sometimes prescribe drugs for us. _____

2. Many people take medicine for an illness. _____

3. Medicines have saved millions of lives. _____

4. Some medicines can be bought over the counter. _____

5. All medicines should be used with supervision. _____

B. Write the prepositional phrase that appears in each sentence.

6. You can make wise choices on health matters.

_____

7. You can gather health information from many sources.

_____

8. Information can be found at your library.

_____

9. You can access information you need from the internet.

_____

10. You know that the best medicine of all is "prevention."

_____

McGraw-Hill Language Arts
Grade 4, Unit 6, Adverbs,
pages 436–437
10

At Home: Write five original sentences using prepositions from Parts A or B.

90

Combining Sentences: Complex Sentences

REMEMBER THE **RULES**

- A **complex sentence** contains two related ideas joined by a conjunction, such as *when, because,* or *unless.*

  Kelly chooses her time wisely. Kelly wants to get good grades.

  *Kelly chooses her time wisely **because** she wants good grades.*

A. Underline the conjunction that connects the two parts of the sentence.

1. Kelly will study hard tonight since she has a test tomorrow.

2. She writes notes on cards because it helps her remember.

3. Kelly tries to recall the information before she looks at the cards.

4. This method usually works unless she writes the wrong notes.

5. She does not take her books wherever she goes.

B. Write one sentence using a conjunction to combine each pair of sentences.

6. Kelly turns off the radio. She is studying.

   _____

7. You can choose to study hard. You want good grades.

   _____

8. School is fun. Our teacher makes it interesting.

   _____

9. I will not do well. I choose to study.

   _____

10. I must study hard. The test is given.

    _____

Mechanics and Usage: Commas

A. Insert commas where they are needed.

1. Karen have you ever read the poem about Paul Revere's Ride?
2. No but I know who wrote it.
3. How did you happen to know about the author Karen?
4. Well the poem is listed in a poetry book I have at home.
5. Please Karen can you bring the book to school?

B. Rewrite each sentence using commas where needed.

6. Oh the poem has to do with the Revolutionary War.

_____

7. Remember class someone had to inform Lexington that the British were coming.

_____

8. Yes Paul Revere warned patriot leaders of their danger.

_____

9. Did you know that Paul Revere rode through the countryside calling men to arms class?

_____

_____

10. Amazingly class Revere's exploits inspired Longfellow to write his poem.

_____

_____

Mixed Review

┌─ **REMEMBER** THE **RULES** ─────────────────────────

- A **negative** means "no." Never use two negatives in a sentence.
- A **preposition** comes before a noun or pronoun and links it to the rest of the sentences. *I enjoy hiking* **with** *friends.*
- A **prepositional phrase** begins with a preposition and ends in a noun or pronoun. *I begin hiking* **in the early morning.**
- **Complex sentences** combine two ideas by using words that tell where, when, why, how, and under what circumstances.

  I enjoy looking for animals **as** *I hike through the forest.*

A. Circle the preposition and underline the prepositional phrase.

1. I really enjoy going on a nature hike.

2. I wake up very early in the morning.

3. Starting with a healthy breakfast is a good idea.

4. I like hiking deep into the forest.

5. The forest is full of interesting sights and sounds.

B. Combine sentence pairs with joining words. Correct the double negatives.

6. I like going on a hike. The weather is nice outside.

   _____

7. I haven't never gone on a hike in winter. The weather is cold.

   _____

8. I take cover in a safe place. The weather turns bad.

   _____

9. I don't make no noise. I want to hear the sounds of the forest.

   _____

10. I like sharing my experiences. My hike is over.

    _____

At Home: Think about some things you have seen in nature. Write five sentences about them. Include some prepositional phrases.

McGraw-Hill Language Arts
Grade 4, Unit 6, Mixed Review,
pages 442–443

10

McGraw-Hill School Division

Common Errors: Adverbs

┌─ **REMEMBER** THE **RULES** ═══════════════════════════

- An **adjective** describes a noun. An **adverb** tells more about a verb.
- **Good** is an adjective. **Well** is an adverb.
  *The heart works **well** at pumping blood through the body.*
- Do not use two negative words together in a sentence.
  *A bad diet doesn't do no̶t̶h̶ing **anything** to help the heart.*
- Remember: Many adverbs can be formed by adding **-ly** to an adjective.
  *The heart **quickly** pumps blood to all parts of the body.*

└───

A. Write the word in parentheses ( ) that completes each sentence correctly.

1. I (recent, recently) read an article about the heart. _____

2. The heart is (constant, constantly) pumping blood. _____

3. The blood flows (swift, swiftly) through the body. _____

4. The heart (actual, actually) beats about 36 million _____

   times a year!

5. Your heart beats (quick, quickly) when you exercise. _____

B. Rewrite each sentence correctly.

6. Doctors can listen close to the sound your heart makes.

   _____

7. Small valves constant regulate the flow of blood.

   _____

8. These valves must work good all the time.

   _____

9. Doctors can quick tell if something is wrong.

   _____

10. The heart doesn't work no more than it has to.

   _____

McGraw-Hill Language Arts
Grade 4, Unit 6, Adverbs
pages 444–445
10

At Home: Write five sentences about how something
works. Use an adverb in each sentence.

94

Study Skills: Encyclopedia

- An **encyclopedia** is a reference work that contains articles on many subjects. Most encyclopedias are made up of a set of books, or volumes.
- The information in an encyclopedia is arranged in the volumes alphabetically by subject.
- The spine of each volume is usually numbered to let you keep each one in order. The spine also has letters or words to tell which part of the alphabet is in that volume.
- The last volume in an encyclopedia is the index, which lists all the subjects written about in the encyclopedia.

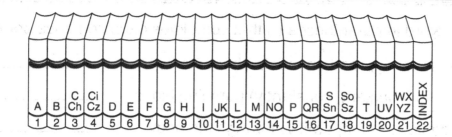

A. Draw a line from the title of an article to the volume of the encyclopedia in which it is found.

1. Julius Caesar	Volume 14
2. how tornadoes form	Volume 4
3. oceanography	Volume 2
4. famous battles of the Civil War	Volume 3
5. how the brain works	Volume 19

B. Write an entry for something interesting you found in the following volumes of the encyclopedias pictured above.

6. A _____   **11.** QR _____

7. B _____   **12.** SSn _____

8. H _____   **13.** SoSz _____

9. JK _____   **14.** UV _____

10. M _____   **15.** WXYZ _____

At Home: List three topics that you would like to know more about. List entry words you think you'll find the topics listed under. Use an encyclopedia to see if you were correct.

95

McGraw-Hill Language Arts Grade 4, Unit 6, Study Skills, pages 452–453   /15

McGraw-Hill School Division

Vocabulary: Suffixes

- A **suffix** is a word part added to the end of a base word. It changes the meaning of the base word.

    Common Suffixes: *able, ible, er, or, ful, less, ly, ment, y*

    wash + able = washable   means "capable of being washed"

    harm + less = harmless   means "without harming anyone or anything"

A. Underline the words with suffixes. Write the words in the box. Then circle the suffixes.

On a rainy day, I like to sit quietly

and work crossword puzzles. Sometimes

I draw colorful pictures. I also get

enjoyment from baking cookies and

listening to music on the radio or

CD player.

1. _____
2. _____
3. _____
4. _____
5. _____

B. Add a suffix to a base word in the box to complete each sentence.

excite	mind	smooth	snow	skate

6. On _____ days, I love to take my sled to the park.

7. I feel such _____ when sliding down a big hill.

8. Dad always reminds us to be _____ of nearby trees or real small kids.

9. I also am an ice _____ .

10. I love to _____ glide across the ice.

McGraw-Hill Language Arts
10 Grade 4, Unit 6, Vocabulary, pages 454–455

At Home: Write a paragraph about what you like to do on a rainy or snowy day. Include five words with suffixes in your work.

96

Composition Skills: Outlining

- An **outline** lists the **main topics** in a report or article.
- Each main idea can be one paragraph in a report.
- Use a **Roman numeral** followed by a **period** before each main topic.
- Each **subtopic** is a detail that supports or explains the main topic.
- Use a **capital letter** followed by a **period** before each subtopic.

A. Leslie jotted down some ideas for a social studies report. The title of her outline is "The United States and Wars: The First 100 Years." Next to each idea, circle whether it should appear as a **main topic** or a **subtopic.**

1. Revolutionary War (1775–1783)   **main topic**   **subtopic**

2. Colonies fight for independence from Britain   **main topic**   **subtopic**

3. War of 1812 (1812–1815)   **main topic**   **subtopic**

4. Trade conflict with Britain   **main topic**   **subtopic**

5. White House burns in 1814   **main topic**   **subtopic**

B. 6-10. Organize Leslie's notes in an outline. In the boxes, write a Roman numeral or capital letter. On the lines, write the information that would be included in this part of the report.

The United States and Wars: The First 100 Years

☐ _____

 ☐ _____

☐ _____

 ☐ _____

 ☐ _____

At Home: Write another main topic that could be included in Leslie's report. See if you can write one or two subtopics for the main topic.

97

McGraw-Hill Language Arts
Grade 4, Unit 6, Composition Skills,
pages 456–457

/10

Features of Expository Writing

> Good expository writing
> - presents a **main idea** based on factual information about a specific topic.
> - includes **supporting details,** including facts, examples, and descriptions.
> - **summarizes** information from a variety of different resources.
> - **draws conclusions** based on the information presented.
> - uses **transitional words and phrases** to connect ideas.

A. Read the paragraph. Underline the sentence that presents the main idea.

1. People can protect nature and help themselves at the same time. For example, salmon swim upstream in rivers to breed and to die. When they cannot make it upstream, they cannot survive. People have built dams on rivers to create low-cost electricity. The dams keep the salmon from making it upstream. What did people in Washington state do? They built steps into the dams, and salmon jump up step-by-step to the water above. Washington state and salmon are in a win-win situation. Finally, the result is new generations of salmon and low-cost electricity for people.

B. Use the paragraph to answer the following questions.

2. What example does the author give to support the main idea?

_____

_____

3. What are two transition words or phrases the author uses in the paragraph?

_____

4. Where is the conclusion stated in the paragraph?

_____

5. Write a summary of this paragraph using one or two sentences.

_____

_____

McGraw-Hill Language Arts
Grade 4, Unit 6, Expository Writing,
5 **pages 464–465**

At Home: How do you feel about protecting nature?
Present information on a topic you are concerned with.
Read your writing to a family member.

97a

Prewrite: Expository Writing

The purpose of **expository writing** is to inform. It requires the writer to use details and facts to support a main idea. Both the writer and his or her readers should be able to draw conclusions about the information presented. **Outlining** is a good way to organize your main ideas and supporting details.

Think of a topic you would like to research and then report on. After you do some research and list ideas about your topic, fill in the outline.

OUTLINE
I.
A.
B.
II.
A.
B.
C.
III.
A.
B.

CHECKLIST

• Have you listed ideas about your topic?

• Have you listed the main ideas and details to support them?

• Do you need to do more research?

At Home: Ask a parent if he or she knows anything about the topic you have chosen. Ask for suggestions on how to find out more about your topic.

97b

McGraw-Hill Language Arts
Grade 4, Unit 6, Expository Writing,
pages 466–469

McGraw-Hill School Division

Revise: Expository Writing

When you **revise** your expository writing, you should check to make sure you have:

- main ideas supported by facts and details
- important information
- a variety of sources
- conclusions about the topic
- transition words, such as *therefore, as a result, for example, on the other hand*

A. Revise the following report by adding a title, main idea, some transition words, and a conclusion.

Some clouds are high in the sky. These are called *cirrus* clouds. Cirrus clouds are thin and look airy. *Cumulus* clouds are white and puffy. They look like soft cotton. These clouds usually float in the middle of the sky. Another kind of cloud is the *stratus*. Stratus clouds look like large sheets. The clouds that bring the rain are called *nimbus*. These clouds sit low over our heads, and they are dark and gray.

Can you guess which cloud type is the coldest? The cirrus clouds are. They are mostly made of ice crystals. Do you know why scientists study clouds?

B. Use another sheet of paper to rewrite the report with your changes.

McGraw-Hill Language Arts
Grade 4, Unit 6, Expository Writing,
pages 472–473

At Home: Write a paragraph about how weather has affected you and your family. Then revise your work.

97c

Proofread: Expository Writing

PROOFREADING MARKS

⌗ new paragraph

∧ add

ℒ take out

≡ Make a capital letter.

/ Make a small letter.

🔘 Check the spelling.

⊙ Add a period.

After you revise your report, you will need to **proofread** it to correct any errors. When you proofread your expository writing you should:

• Read to make sure your subjects and verbs agree.

• Add commas to separate items in a series and after introductory phrases.

• Check for capitalization of proper nouns and other punctuation.

• Combine short sentences.

• Check for spelling errors.

A. Read the following expository writing. Use the proofreading marks from the box to mark any errors you find.

Have you ever heard the term *air pressure* when you listen to a

weather report on radio or TV Air pressure play an important role in

weather. If the air pressue is rising, it means that the weather is going to

improve. When air pressure falls bad weather may be on its way. most

storms happen in low-pressure areas. Scientists measure air pressure.

Scientists use a barometer

Air is all around us. It pushes against us all the time. I did an

experiment with air to find out just how strong it is. I used a ruler a table,

and a sheet of paper. I put the ruler on the table so that about 1/3 of it

stuck over the edge. Then I put the paper over the ruler. Next, I hit the

ruler to try to make the paper flie into the air. Guess what happened

B. Rewrite the paragraphs with your changes on another sheet of paper.

At Home: Clip a short paragraph from a newspaper. Ask a family member to rewrite it on a sheet of paper without the punctuation. Then punctuate that paragraph.

97d

McGraw-Hill Language Arts
Grade 4, Unit 6, Expository Writing,
pages 476–477

10

McGraw-Hill School Division